Tales of an Inland
Empire Girl

What people are saying about

Tales of an Inland Empire Girl

"In her first novel, Juanita E. Mantz goes back to the old house to unshackle the ghosts that still inhabit the charred curtains and broken windows of her youth. We meet the Wonder Twins, a Wolfman Jack stand in, The Flintstones, a young Wonder Woman with tinfoil wristbands & Nancy Drew incognito via unexpected introductions into Mantz's life growing up in The Inland Empire. This is as creative as autobiography gets without veering from the hard truths herein. Maybe you saw the cartoon once, and thought it fantasy, but read this book and then firmly believe that underdogs can fly."
— Dennis Callaci, author of *100 Cassettes*

"*Tales of an Inland Empire Girl* is a searing, beautiful memoir that illuminates the struggles of parents who are beaten down by life and their arduous working-class jobs and of children who are trapped in the middle of their parents' battles. A compelling read — raw, honest, and hopeful. I wish this book existed when I was growing up. It would have been my life preserver."
— liz gonzález, author of *Dancing in the Santa Ana Winds*

"In *Tales of an Inland Empire Girl* we know we are in for a bumpy ride from the very opening pages of the first story, 'A Shit Day,' which recounts the author's journey home to Southern California's less-than-glamorous Inland Empire from her high-powered attorney life in San Francisco, arriving at grungy 'Ontario, the kind of airport no one wants go to.' The purpose of this visit: her father is dying. From this gripping opening, Mantz takes readers into a deeper journey of a childhood and coming of age filled with turbulence and tight-knit family love, and she

writes with blazing grit, flashing joy-de-vivre, and an occasional comic overtone that feels natural coming from this self-professed punk-rock girl. This collection of stories spares no stone unturned, no watershed truth - both hard and celebratory - unexamined. And through it all, shines an anthem call of what matters most in life: the unbreakable bonds of family, and this family's enduring love for one another."
— Ruth Nolan, born in the IE and editor of *No Place for a Puritan: the Literature of California's Deserts*

"Tales of an Inland Empire Girl, set in the fast-growing Eastern region of Southern California and told in Mantz's smack-in-your-face honesty, lures one into the places of childhood—of first home and lasting memories. One learns to live, however awkward life might be, in a house 'the color of dirt', finding a place to call one's own in a Plastic Cheese chair, and love, even through girl fights. Through dexterous use of language, Mantz tosses her readers into a reality where a little girl finds herself in tears of frustration and shame with two left shoes, a drunken dad and screaming mom, but loves deeply anyway, and deals with her situations with twin-powered bravado and punk rock: 'I feel as if I could dance forever,' says Mantz."
— Hồng-Mỹ Basrai, author of *Behind the Red Curtain*

"*Tales of an Inland Empire Girl* is deep and funny and true. A remarkable story of resilience and love told in bright prose, and written from a place of rigorous vulnerability that draws us in from the start."
— Brett Paesel, author of *Los Angeles Times* bestseller, *Mommies Who Drink*

Acknowledgments

The author gratefully acknowledges the publications in which earlier versions of the following stories originally appeared:

"A Shit Day" in *The Inlandia Journal*

"Grandpa's House" in *The Acentos Review*

"Movie Time" in *As/Us: A Space for Writers of the World*

"My Tia Tilly" in *Muse*

"Weaving Roads" in *The James Franco Review*

"Two Left Shoes" in *Hispanecdotes*

Tales of an Inland Empire Girl

Juanita E. Mantz

Los Nietos Press
Downey California
2022

Published in the United States by
Los Nietos Press
Downey, CA 90240
www.LosNietosPress.com
LosNietosPress@gmail.com

Cover and interior photos courtesy of the author.
Inland Empire Cover Photo: Wikipedia user Amerique.
Used under the Creative Commons Attribution-Share Alike
2.0 Generic license,
https://creativecommons.org/licenses/by-sa/2.0/legalcode.

First Edition
ISBN-13: 978-1-7356984-3-4

Dedication

For my parents, John and Judy. Thank you for working so hard and loving us so much.

For my Wonder Twin Jackie and my little sister Annie. Thank you both for being such a big part of the story of my life.

To my big sister Roberta. You are such a part of this.

Finally, for my husband Adrian. Dearest Adrian, my love, there is a light that will never go out.

Contents

"I always tell people that I became a writer not because I went to school but because my mother took me to the library."

Sandra Cisneros

Prologue

A Shit Day

The day starts out bad. Like bad days always do, it gets worse. Ontario Airport is where it starts. Ontario Airport is the kind of airport no one wants to go to, in the middle of nowhere. Ontario is known as the apex of the Inland Empire ("the IE"), which is like being called King Shit on Turd Island. The IE is where my parents had lived for years and where I grew up. Our house was the notorious one where all the screaming and yelling came from, the bright red-and-blue lights of the police cars signaling our family's dysfunction for our neighbors.

I had taken the week off from my attorney gig at a large law firm in San Francisco to see my dad, who was sick. Later, after everything has changed, I will leave corporate law forever to become a deputy public defender, but this is before.

My twin sister Jackie picks me up at the airport. We fight sometimes, knock-down-drag-out fights, but Jackie and I are close. We are so close that we call ourselves the Wonder Twins. Mom said we had our own language as kids and that we read each other's minds.

I decide that the only way to help Dad feel better is to get him some fish. Some people think of fish and picture broiled sole or freshly grilled halibut. In my family, we like Long John Silvers. Their fish is the ultimate in fast-food processed crispy deliciousness, and their fish basket comes with their deep-fried hush puppy potatoes.

Food equals comfort in my family, and the more fried the better. We hit the Long John Silvers on Mountain in Ontario and pick up the fish. Jackie and I walk up to my parent's apartment in Mira Loma, greasy bag of fish in hand. Before I ring the bell, Mom opens the door with a sullen-sounding grunt. Mom is not mysterious. She wears her anger on her sleeve like most people wear their hearts.

"What took you so goddamn long?" Mom says as she walks past me. "Watch your dad. I need a new cell phone." She leaves with a squeal of her car's tires without looking back.

Here we are, Jackie, me and Dad. I give Dad the fish. He doesn't want to eat it. He has lost so much weight that he looks like a little bird. Dad used to be a big guy and now he is bone-thin in his white T-shirt. I feel a rock in my chest and cannot breathe for a moment when I see him.

I make Dad eat the fish. I admit it, I make him. I am the oldest twin, and Jackie and our younger sister Annie call me the bossy one, and I call Jackie the fucked-up middle child, and Jackie and I call Annie the spoiled baby. I admit I boss him into it. I say, "Dad, eat the fish, you'll feel better." He nods.

Dad takes one bite of the fish and starts choking. Jackie and I look at each other. What are we going to do? We communicate with looks, not saying anything. We can read each other's minds like I said.

Time stands still for a moment. Dad is choking. It seems as if he is choking to death, and I think to myself, *He's gonna die from that goddamn piece of fish that I made him eat.*

With just instinct guiding me, I run outside and scream into the air, "Help! Help me, someone!"—and then out of nowhere help arrives.

A man comes running from the golf course next door— and, mind you, it's a crappy, unkempt, nine-hole golf course. The man has a UC Riverside hat on. The guy must be in his sixties but is spry as hell for a senior. He runs into the house like Superman. Usually I would be embarrassed for someone to see my parents' messy house, but I am grateful.

Superman doesn't hesitate. He grabs Dad out of the hospice bed and gives him the Heimlich maneuver, and the piece of fried fish flies out and hits the wall. We all just stand there for a moment, Jackie, myself, Dad, and old-man Superman. Superman disappears before I can say thank you, and Dad looks at me with his blue eyes and says with a grunt, "You almost killed me, Jenny."

Jackie and I laugh but I think, *He's right, I almost killed him. I did.* This is the moment I realize that Dad is going to die. No, I didn't kill him with the fish, but the cancer is going to take him. It has to. You don't get that sick, you're not on hospice care, unless you are going to die. Even Superman can't fix that.

A couple of hours later, Mom comes home, and my younger sister Annie walks in the door with her kids Selena and Sophie. Selena, who is six, hugs Dad a hard goodbye. "Love you, grandpa," she says. Annie holds baby Sophie up to Dad for him to kiss, and he nuzzles her fingers and smiles. Dad is back to himself for a moment.

Annie leaves and now it is me, Mom, and Jackie sitting with Dad. Really it is just me because my mom and Jackie are useless. Jackie is texting and Mom is in her bedroom reading one of her Harlequin romance novels. Mom has always loved those stupid dime-store romance novels. When we were little, Mom had a whole library of them and would let Jackie and me read them even though we were still in elementary school. Dad built her bookshelves in the garage to house all of the white paperbacks. Maybe right now the fantasies are comforting.

The bathing nurse arrives. Dad says he has to use the bathroom and the nurse takes him to the bathroom. I watch as he walks slowly with her help into the bathroom.

Then I hear the bathing nurse scream, "Help me, Help me!"

Dad dies right there on the toilet, his pants around his ankles like fucking Elvis. I don't know it at the time, but I find out later that a lot of people die on the toilet. It's because when you take a shit your blood pressure drops. And his incompetent, Medicare-provided bathing nurse doesn't know CPR.

There are no angels singing. There is no beautiful,

Hallmark, last-breath kind of moment. Just him on the toilet. What a shitty way to die.

The rest is a rush like a Twilight Zone movie on fast forward. Surreal and real at the same time.

I call 911 screaming, "Please help me. My father, he's not breathing."

My voice doesn't sound like my own. The paramedics screech up in mere minutes. I time it while crying, looking down at my watch, hyperventilating outside in the cool Riverside air.

When the paramedics get inside, they start CPR. They don't seem hopeful. After about five minutes, one of the male paramedics asks me, "Should we go on?"

That is when I know I am going to be the one to decide whether to let Dad go. Am I going to let him go? Can I do this? I don't know. Can I let my dad go? I keep asking myself in my mind over and over. What should I do?

As one paramedic's fingers thump into Dad's chest and the other breathes into his mouth, they ask me again, for the second time, "Should we go on?"

Dad looks like a bloated fish lying there. My mind flashes back to that fried fish from earlier. That damn fish basket is haunting me. I look back down at my dad. He isn't breathing—they are making him breathe, but he isn't breathing.

The paramedic looks at me for a third time and says, "Should we go on?" I look at Mom. We stare at each other and she is crying, tears running down her face. Mom grabs at me and hugs me tight for what feels like the first time in my whole life, except maybe when I was a baby. She must have hugged me when I was a baby, right?

Mom and I moan into each other's arms while Jackie sits outside against a tree texting.

Jackie is standing against the tree with that vacant-house look she gets on her face, like she's not there. Our dad is dying, and she can't help me. Mom can't help me. What the hell should I do?

"Should we go on?" the paramedics ask me again.

Thoughts race through my head. I don't want to do this. Why do I have to do this? Is it because I am the oldest? If you want to be technical, I am not the oldest. Jackie and I are twins. I am a thirty-something lawyer. I am also the high-school dropout in my family, as Mom reminds me periodically. My route to USC Law was a detour rather than a straight path after I royally fucked up high school. This straight-A student ditched and dozed her way through her senior year. You see, all that childhood chaos had to go somewhere. I am like an ABC Afterschool Special, one titled: "How to Make It Through a Crazy Childhood Intact."

Where the hell is Annie? She always gets out of everything. When Mom would go batshit crazy when we were little, Annie never got hit. Annie always hid under the bed. Now, when I need her, she's not here. Annie was the baby who always got everything she wanted. Annie got the cherry-apple bike; us twins got the yellow banana bikes and they called Jackie and me the banana-bike twins. She got the white fur coat, we got the dark brown fur coats. Why does Annie get out of it? Why am I stuck with this burden? Annie is the lucky one.

Then one of the paramedics asks me again, for what

must have been the fifth time, "Should we go on?" They are going on. One female paramedic is breathing into Dad's mouth and the male paramedic is pumping Dad's heart with his hands. Dad is just lying there.

I flash back to when I was little, Dad driving in his truck listening to Johnny Cash on the eight-track, smoking a Kent cigarette, one hand on the wheel, his beer in a green foam sleeve.

Standing there, I remember Dad on the barbecue in the backyard making us steaks. I picture lying out by the pool at our Ontario house and all of us together as a family. I can see Dad at his bar, The Big O, racking the balls on the pool table and playing pinball with me and my sisters on a Saturday morning. I picture Dad in his pickup truck taking us to the drive-in movie theater. I remember when Dad lost his bar, then the house, and the day our half-sister Barb died when we were in high school. I shake my head remembering him trying to hug me, how I always shook him off.

I think about the good times and the bad. I think back to all of the fighting and all of that childhood chaos. When Dad got drunk, he and Mom would fight like maniacs. I grew up in a war zone of sorts, but there were good times. I always blamed Dad for everything, and it wasn't all his fault. Dad was a drunk, but Mom was crazy when she got angry. Despite all of the chaos, Dad stayed. He stayed.

There were some great times. I think about fishing in Montana when we were little, and our road trips, especially the one to Flintstones Land.

Why do I always focus on the bad stuff? Why haven't I been here to see him more often? What am I running from?

Why am I trying to be someone else? A high-powered lawyer who never sees her family.

Dad was always there for me, even if he was drunk. A drunk dad is better than no dad at all. I remember Dad playing cards with us when Mom had to work late at the restaurant. Dad would always wake up early to make me and my sisters breakfast every Saturday and Sunday morning. Bacon so crispy it would crumble in your mouth. Pancakes with jelly inside, or fried bologna and eggs. Dad was always there.

I jump back to present day as the paramedic asks the question again, "Should we go on?"

I take a deep breath and then another and let go one word:

"No."

***

I watch as they cover Dad's body. Everyone is quiet like in church. Dad is gone. He is dead. The word repeats in my head like a prayer. I already miss Dad's voice saying my name. It is almost like I can still hear him saying it. Am I imagining it or is that his voice whispering in my head?

There is still so much I want to say to him. I want to see him again, alive.

Shaking my head, I sigh and listen to Mom weeping. Jackie paces outside, gazing up into the sky. We call Annie and tell her. She is on her way. It is dark outside now.

They wheel Dad's body out. My heart stops, or at least it feels like it does—maybe it just breaks. Tears run down my face and I wipe them away. I have so much regret. I can almost taste it.

Reeling, I fall into my head and go back, to the beginning. I have to figure this out. Who was I, who am I, and who do I want to be? I have to start at the beginning. I have to remember.

> *"Memory fades, memory adjusts, memory conforms
> to what we think we remember."*
> Joan Didion

Flintstones Land

Mom and Dad fight the whole way from California. They fight about which way to turn and where to go. They fight about when to eat and they fight about us kids causing a ruckus. Mom gets mad because Dad always likes to take the long way. Dad uses a Thomas Guide, which is a big book full of maps. The only time Mom and Dad aren't bickering is when Dad turns on the country station and they sing along to Waylon Jennings and Willie Nelson, with me and my sisters snapping our fingers to the beat.

We are driving to Flintstones Land in South Dakota. Mom and Dad are here for my sister Roberta's wedding in Jefferson. Dad says we came to South Dakota so we could see Mount Rushmore, too. That's the super-high mountain of rocks with the presidents' faces carved in it. We also visit a cave where you could see a bunch of crystals hanging from the ceiling. It is so pretty.

On the road, I stare out the window and me and Jackie play the alphabet game, watching signs for A to Z. We stop at Motel 6 to sleep. We all share a room and eat McDonald's for dinner.

I can't believe it when I see Flintstones Land. I yelp in happiness. The Flintstones are one of our favorite cartoons. We are staying in Dad's pickup truck in the RV park next door, sleeping in the back of the shell on packing blankets.

I am riding Dino the dinosaur. I am playing with my sisters in a rock house. I am full of joy.

Flintstones Land is magic. It's everything. It's so colorful and bright, just like the cartoon. Jackie and I climb into a rock car that has rock wheels. We pretend we are at the Flintstones drive-in movie theater and that the car is about to tip over from the weight of a brontosaurus steak. Annie begs to get in but we ignore her.

Dad yells "Yabba dabba do!" He raises his fist in the air and smiles. Mom winces, shakes her head, and smiles. She is trying to let go and have fun.

This is before Dad wrecked his legs from moving furniture for far too long. This is before all the years of Dad's smoking and beer drinking took their toll. This is when Mom is working only one waitressing job and times are good. My parents are still "bill-poor," as Mom will say, but there is enough money for this vacation.

Flintstones Land is even better than Disneyland to us as kids. The park shines in my mind, an image imprinted there to drown out all the bad days. I tell myself, Remember all the good times. There were many good times. Remember? Why do you always focus on the bad times? Remember the good, remember, remember....

What I remember most are the rocks. There were lots

of colored houses made of rocks. Everything was made of rocks, including all the Flintstones cars and the tables. There were painted signs with images of all the characters. It was the opposite of high tech, and when I tell people about it now they do not believe it existed. It will take me years to try to write about it. As an adult, I will not fully believe it existed, as if it was a figment of my imagination, until my twin sister Jackie visits it with my mom right before it closes for good in 2019. Jackie buys me a Flintstones Land T-shirt. But let's get back to then, and to my memories before they glide away.

Here is what I remember. There were statues of all of the characters, with places you could put your head through to take a picture. I imagine that I put my head through Bam Bam and then Dino and ignored Betty and Pebbles as too girly. As a kid, I want to "bam bam bam" like Bam Bam rather than wear a dress and pearls.

Dad peeks his head out through Fred Flintstone. Mom peeks through Wilma. I point my fingers like two guns at Dad, yelling my favorite rhyme, "Bang Bang! You're dead, brush your teeth and go to bed!"

Despite all the arguments and fights, my parents are beautiful at that age. Mom's thick hair is in an updo like a beehive and she's wearing shorts and a striped shirt. Her skinny legs are dark brown from tanning at the beach. Dad's in his thirties, with his big belly hanging over his wrangler jeans, topped off by a blue shirt and a bolo tie. His cowboy hat is in the pickup truck. Dad's smiling again and pulling out his false teeth to make us all laugh. I watch Mom laugh as Dad tickles her and slaps his knee, crossing his eyes as he ogles her.

My sisters and I run around Flintstones Land screaming and giggling. Mom and Dad eat Wonder Bread bologna sandwiches from a Styrofoam cooler. We slurp Shasta colas out of cans to quench our thirst. The soda is so cold it burns my eyes. I wipe the orange bubbles off my chin and grin.

Writing this story, I think I want to reach out and make us all hold hands. Sentimental, I know, but so needed.

Flower Girls

We prepare to walk into the church for my sister Roberta's wedding. Mom grabs my arm and says with her you-better-listen face, "Behave." Jackie is starting to giggle. I look at her and nudge her quiet. We are flower girls. Our dresses make us look like farm girls from another era; shiny, pale white caps cover our ears. "They look like the caps the cafeteria ladies wear," Jackie says.

"Those twins," Roberta mumbles. "Nothing but a pile of double trouble."

Everyone is looking at us, the twins, as we walk down the center aisle practicing for the real thing. We twins are a handful. Roberta loves our sister Annie the best. Everyone loves Annie. Roberta can't stop playing with her. They even look alike with their pale skin and long, straight brown hair. Jackie and I are brown berries with untamable frizzy hair. Annie is a "mini" flower girl, and of course her dress rivals Cinderella's, all froth and tulle.

At least I remember it that way.

Roberta is only seventeen and is marrying Chuck, her high-school sweetheart. Dad has to sign for her. Roberta's mother Tiny also has to sign under Dakota law. Roberta is only our half-sister, a fact my mother keeps reminding us of. Tiny was Dad's first wife. "That Tiny," Mom always says with a scowl. She says it again in the dressing room right before the wedding. Dad's blue eyes blink rapidly behind his thick glasses. He whispers, "Judy! SHHHHH! Roberta will hear you."

That only makes Mom madder. She looks at Dad with a glare and whispers, "I don't fucking care. You better not talk to her at the reception."

Now we are in the church for real. As we walk down the aisle, I feel Jackie pinch my arm. "Ouch," I whisper and nudge Jackie with my elbow. Mom is glaring at us as we walk side by side down the center aisle toward the front of the church, as the sound of the organ fills my ears. During the service Jackie pinches me, not once, not twice, but three times a lady. Over and over—it doesn't stop. I try to slap her away discreetly. It's no use. I feel Roberta glance our way occasionally through her veil. She looks worried. She should be. I am.

I think, *I can't take it anymore.* My arm feels like it is black and blue, and at the exact moment Roberta is about to say "I do," I step away from Jackie's side and put Annie in between us. Later there will be hell to pay.

Two Left Shoes

"Goddammit, Jackie," Mom screams at my twin sister, who is sitting in the back seat behind me. We're in the parking lot at the elementary school. Mom has parked under a tall tree that covers us in its shadow. The kids in other cars are staring at us. I scrunch down in the front seat.

"How could you do this?" Mom's screaming gets louder as she glares at Jackie, who has her head down. Jackie will never cry in front of Mom no matter how loud she screams. When Mom hits her, Jackie stays still like a statue. This is her tree stance. Jackie doesn't even blink. I know if I cry, it makes the hitting stop, but Jackie is stubborn. I think Mom picks on Jackie because she is Dad's favorite.

Jackie is wearing her favorite rainbow shirt with her sky-blue, flared Dittos, and her curly brown hair is in two ponytails with purple barrettes. I am wearing my favorite green frog shirt with green Ditto flares. My hair is in ponytails with pink barrettes. We usually dress exactly alike, but today I wanted to wear my lucky shirt.

"You know I have to drop Annie off and go to work." Mom is a waitress and can't be late. She says her boss is a son of a bitch. Her feet always hurt. Mom's always running around and always working, taking care of us kids, looking for Dad at the bars when he gets off work. Mom's always tired.

Jackie has on two left shoes. One of mine and one of hers. I feel bad. It's not her fault our tennis shoes are alike and that she's left-handed and gets things mixed up, just like her backwards Bs and Ds. If I had worn my tennis shoes instead of my brown sandals, everything would have been fine.

My stomach hurts. I open my Ramona book. I love reading about the sisters Ramona and Beezus. Ramona is my age and she drives her older sister Beezus crazy when she blows bubbles through straws. I love books. Mom says I would read anything, even a cereal box. She tells me to read everything I can.

Our baby sister Annie is also in the back seat. Annie's face is all red as if she is about to howl. Mom drives away with a screech and slaps at Jackie in the back seat but doesn't reach her. Mom has only one hand on the wheel. Jackie taps me and looks at me with her "Help me" face. I always know what she is thinking. Mom said we had our own language when we were babies. I focus on her and think, get the right shoe and get it quick.

Mom drives back to the house like a maniac. Our house has Zs on the windows and Dad has planted pink geraniums in the front yard. We have a basement where we can read and play games. Mom says she hates living on the same street as Montclair High School because the kids throw stuff on the lawn, like soda cans and used candy wrappers.

I get carsick from the car swerving and can't read my book. Sometimes, Mom is like the witch from "Hansel and Gretel" when she scares us. Maybe Jackie is Cinderella and Mom is the wicked stepmother, except she is our real mom. That would make Dad a prince.

Mom jerks the car to a stop at the curb, swivels her head, and screams at Jackie, "Get in that house and find that shoe!" Mom's eyes shine like big black buttons. Jackie runs into the house. I want to follow her to get away from Mom, but I can't leave Annie alone with her, not when she's in this mood. When Mom is like this she shouldn't drive. Annie is her baby and her favorite, but I still get scared Mom will crash.

Mom mutters to herself, cursing, "I am gonna be fucking late."

I lean over to the back seat and grab at Annie's hands so she won't cry, which will make things worse because Mom can't stand crying. She says Annie is a good baby because she rarely cries. Mom says all we twins did was cry when we were babies.

Annie thinks I am trying to play patty-cake and lifts her hands in the air and giggles. Mom looks at me and her eyes are not as dark. Nice Mom is coming back. Her eyes turn from dark to kind and she pats my shoulder.

Jackie emerges from our house a minute later, one foot bare, a shoe in hand. Her face is all red, her eyes blotchy. Jackie jumps into the back seat and starts putting on the shoe. Mom revs the engine and pulls away from the curb. Jackie ties the laces and taps my shoulder and whispers, "Is this right, Jenny?" I lean over the seat and look down at her feet and whisper back, "Yeah, you're good." Mom turns her head and pats Jackie on the head while driving.

We fist-bump like our favorite superheroes, the Wonder Twins. The Wonder Twins' secret power is to bump fists and morph. "Wonder Twin powers, activate!" Wonder Twin Jayna can morph into an animal and Wonder Twin Zan can change into water or ice. Jackie and I touch fists and whisper in unison, "Form of a good day."

We are back at school in less than five minutes. Mom walks us into the office, holding Annie by the hand. "Sorry they're late. This one put on two left shoes," she says with a smile to the office receptionist. The nice mom, our real mom, the one who acts like the mom from "The Brady Bunch," is back. The receptionist walks us each into our separate classes and, as Jackie walks by me, I give her a thumbs-up. Her eyes are watery, so I pat her shoulder. I hold out my fist and Jackie holds out hers and we fist-bump again. Jackie turns and smiles and I say, "Bye, Wonder Twin." Jackie shakes her head but when I shake my head back and wink, she smiles.

Trading Places

Everyone thinks my twin sister Jackie and I look exactly alike. The doctor told Mom that we are "mirror twins" because I am right-handed and Jackie is left-handed. We look so much alike that we can fool people when we want to, even Mom and Dad.

Jackie and I have tan skin and brown hair and eyes. Jackie weighs five more pounds than I do and she has two dimples and I only have one. We both have Mom's curly hair which Mom says comes from our Mexican side. Our younger sister Annie looks like Dad with her straight hair and light skin. Dad was born in Montana and Mom always says he comes from poor white trash and that his own dad was very mean to him.

His family was so poor that Dad was in an orphanage when he was little. His parents couldn't feed their kids, so they put him and his brother and sister in an orphanage in Montana for a couple of years. Dad said it was really bad. They made him eat rice all the time. His parents died years ago. We never met them.

I am in Mrs. G's kindergarten class. She is a fat, white

woman with a tight bun and a sharp ruler that she is not afraid to use. I saw her use the ruler before, but never on me. I am always the good girl in class. I sit in the front row and love to answer questions.

The teachers say I read a lot for my age. Mom taught Jackie and me to read when we were three. Mom taught us to read by sitting with us at our small kitchen table for hours, watching us as we sounded out words. She would drink cup after cup of coffee.

Now that I can read, Mom sometimes lets me read her Harlequin romances. They are like fairy tales with real people. The books use words like ravished and swooned which can be confusing, but I can usually figure out what the words mean. Some days, I want to live inside the books, especially when Mom and Dad are fighting.

This is our second year in kindergarten. Last year, the school held us back because Jackie turns her Bs into Ds and we were only four when we started. Now we are five, almost six. Mom says I had to repeat kindergarten, too, because we are twins and it would have been bad for Jackie if she got held back and I didn't.

They call me Jenny in class even though my real name is Juanita. I've always been called Jenny by my family. I like the nickname Jenny but would prefer they call me Lynda. Lynda Carter is Wonder Woman's real name and I want to be just like her. She's half white and half Mexican just like me. She's one of my favorite superheroes, and Dad watches her show on television all the time. Jackie and I make fake bracelets out of foil and use towels for capes and pretend to be her throwing our hair and raising our wrists at one another and kicking high into the air twirling an invisible lasso.

Jackie's teacher is Mrs. S. All the kids call Mrs. S "Big Bird" because Mrs. S is six feet tall with long blonde hair. Her class is the fun one, filled with laughing children and finger painting. Mrs. S plays the piano, and their class is like being in the Girl Scouts where they sit around the campfire singing. Mrs. S eats at the Chinese restaurant where Mom works. She comes in every Friday with her husband. Mrs. S likes Jackie and when she goes to eat at Mom's restaurant, she tells Mom how nice and sweet Jackie is.

Jackie is a different person under the shade of Mrs. S. Jackie and Mom always butt heads. Jackie will never give in and make Mom happy.

The switch is Jackie's idea even though later she will say it wasn't. The night before the switch, we are in our room. I am reading one of Mom's Harlequin romance novels. I can't figure out all the words, but the book gives me a warm feeling in my stomach.

Jackie's reading *Are You There God? It's Me, Margaret*. I already read it. We ordered it from the Scholastic catalogue. Jackie is laughing out loud.

Jackie starts chanting, "I must, I must, I must increase my bust."

Jackie always wants my attention when I am doing something. I yell at her, "Shut up, Jackie, you're being a pain. I'm reading."

She goes quiet and I can tell I hurt her feelings.

A minute later, out of nowhere, she says, "Jenny, lets switch classes tomorrow. It'll be fun."

I shake my head at least three times, but then give in and say, "Fine, but we better not get caught. Let's wear the same clothes."

Wearing the same clothes is not hard because all our clothes match anyway. This will be another of our twin adventures. We sometimes like to trick people, then act out the story to each other over and over like in a movie.

It is Monday morning and Jackie and I walk with each other to our classrooms. Jackie is nervous.

"It will be fine, Jackie," I say and give her a high five as we part ways.

Jackie slaps my hand and says with a giggle, "Good luck, Jenny. Oops... I mean Jackie."

Mrs. S is busy cleaning up the room when I walk in and she looks at me and says, "Good morning, Jackie."

I smile at her, willing myself to smile wide like Jackie. Mrs. S is so nice. Even though it is a math day, I don't mind. Mrs. S is sweet where Ms. G is sour, and Mrs. S is calm, unlike Ms. G, who is always marching around the room, ruler in hand.

I am doing good pretending at being Jackie. Every time Mrs. S says the name "Jackie" I look up and answer. After lunch break, I almost forget where I am and think to myself, we are getting away with it.

The afternoon is almost over when the door to the class opens and Mrs. G stomps into Mrs. S's classroom. The two kindergarten classes are right next door to each other. Mrs. G scowls and whispers something in Mrs. S's ear and points at Jackie, who is standing right outside the open door. Then Mrs. G points at me. *Oh no*, I think. *This isn't good.*

Mrs. S shakes her head, but I see the hint of a smile on her lips, almost like she finds it funny.

Mrs. S walks over and whispers in my ear, "Jenny, go back to your own class. It will be fine."

I get up and Mrs. S crooks her finger at Jackie, who walks in and sits down in my former seat. I see Mrs. S place her hand on Jackie's shoulder. I try to catch Jackie's eye, but she is looking down at the ground.

Mrs. G has me by my T-shirt. I am so scared I feel like I might pee myself. I dig my nails into my hand. Why did we do this? What if I get suspended? Mom is going to kill me.

Mrs. G doesn't say a word as she marches me back to class. We walk into her classroom. I stand at the front of the class. Mrs. G scowls and says, "Stand here, Jenny," motioning to the space next to the piano.

Mrs. G takes out her ruler and holds it up in the air. She doesn't say a word. Then she takes my right hand and puts it on top of the piano and hits my knuckles with her ruler. Red welts pop up.

My classmates let out a collective "Ohhh."

With the crack of the wood on my skin, I am no longer the good twin.

This is all Jackie's fault, her with her stupid ideas. My eyes start to water. I put my head on my desk. Looking up at the clock, I can't wait for class to be over. For once, I don't pay attention to the lesson and just stare out the window. My face is hot. Time goes slow and when the bell rings, I walk out of class with a quick step, staring at the ground. Hand over my eyes, I wait for Mom at the corner and don't say a word as Jackie comes up.

"They said she hit you. Is that true, Jenny?" Jackie says. She is frowning and I know she feels bad. Squinting at her, I nod and my eyes start to water again. "It was my fault, Jenny," Jackie says, her mouth in a straight line. "All my fault. I made a black cat for the Halloween party and when I wrote your name on the back, I reversed the J. I'm so sorry, Wonder Twin."

I shake my head at her without saying a word. It figures, Jackie and her stupid backwards letters.

When Mom picks us up, Jackie jumps in the back seat. She can't help herself. "Mom, you won't believe what happened, Jenny and I switched classes…."

"You what?" Mom says. Mom's eyes get small and her lips scrunch up. She is about to blow up. Jackie knows she messed up, and tries to change the subject. "Yeah, Mom, and guess what, Mrs. G hit Jenny."

I hold up my red-knuckled fingers. Already I know what is coming.

"What? She hit you?" Mom says as she steps on the brakes and swerves the car to a halt against the curb.

"Let's go," Mom says, getting out of the car. She pulls my door open and I hunch out of the car. Jackie stays in the car.

Running, I can barely keep up with Mom as she sprints back toward the school. She is on her break from the restaurant and I keep my eye on her white waitressing shoes. I follow her as she marches down to my kindergarten classroom, arms waving at her sides, muttering under her breath.

I plead with her not to embarrass me. "Mom, I'm fine,

don't say anything, please, Mom, please!" Mom ignores me.

As she crosses the threshold of the classroom, Mom gets right in Mrs. G's face.

Mom spits out her words. Her spit hits Mrs. G's glasses. Mrs. G takes off her glasses and puts them in her pocket and wrings her hands.

Mom screams, "Don't you ever touch my child again or you'll be sorry."

Mrs. G backs up against the piano. "I'm sorry, Mrs. Mantz. I'm sorry. It won't happen again. I'm so sorry. I apologize."

Mrs. G goes from a towering giant to a shrinky-dink within seconds. Ask anyone—when Mom's mad, she can make the devil wet himself. We walk out of the room and I turn and shake my head at Mrs. G in a "You did not know who you were messing with" kind of way. Looking into her red face and round eyes, I almost feel bad for her.

Mom tells the principal off that day, too. We walk down to the administration building. "Don't say a word, Jenny," Mom warns. I know she means it. Mom is still mad as a hatter. Her big shoes clomp as she walks.

Mom looks at the principal's secretary and says in her Nice Mom voice, "May we speak with the principal?" The secretary shakes her head and says, "He's on the phone." Mom's face turns almost purple. She waves her hand at the lady and we barge into the principal's office. Mom screams at the principal, "I'm the only one that can hit my kids."

"I will sue you and your district," Mom yells, waving her hand in the principal's face. "You did not have my permission to use corporal punishment on my child." Mom bangs her fist on his desk. I don't know what corporal punishment is, but it sounds like a big deal.

Mom says. "I may be a waitress, but I am not dumb. That white teacher hit my kid! Who the hell does that pendeja think she is?"

The staff is milling around his door. Sweat drips down the principal's face as he walks us out, still apologizing. He tells Mom that he will meet with Mrs. G right away.

Mrs. G tiptoes around me for the rest of the year. I may not be the good girl anymore, but at least I am the bad girl with a badass mom. The universe does compensate. Sometimes it sucks having a crazy mom. Then sometimes it's not so bad.

Girl Fight

My first girl fight was in elementary school and I got my butt whipped big time. The girl I fought was small but super quick. I was standing in the back of Mariposa Elementary's playground with a ring of people around us, and the girl socked me in the face at least three times in rapid succession. I didn't even try to fight back. The kids booed with displeasure. At some point, the girl must have felt sorry for me and stopped the fight.

My second fight was in high school, sophomore year. I was still transitioning out of my nerdy phase. My opponent was a badass, heavyset chola who I will call Carla, who wore her hair straight up, blow-dried with Aqua Net. Her little sister and I got into an argument, and I talked trash to Carla when she confronted me on her little sister's behalf. Carla told me to meet her in South Quad after school. Word got around quick, and Jackie, who could throw down with the best of them, ran up to me at lunch and told me she had heard about the pending fight.

Jackie looked at me and said, "You can't fight her, Jenny. That girl is tough. She'll kick your ass." She was right.

I sighed, "I know." Jackie continued to lecture me, "Dammit, Jenny, why do you always have to talk shit if you can't back it up?" I didn't say anything. Jackie hesitated and then shrugged her shoulders. "Fuck it, I'll fight her for you."

We walked to South Quad after school and Jackie and that girl were going at it, blow after blow, for what seemed like twelve rounds. Jackie totally held her own. I closed my eyes at some point and, when it was all over, the general consensus was that the fight was a draw. Jackie's only battle scar was a deep scratch down her face because the girl had raked her nails, which had been sharpened to a point, down Jackie's face.

I don't remember if I hugged Jackie, but I should have, because she saved me a serious ass-kicking. She was so fearless. I could always talk a lot of shit, but Jackie was the true fighter.

The King Chair

I am in our family room watching "What's Happening" on our Zenith television. Roger's little sister Dee is telling her brother to give her a quarter to keep her mouth shut.

Our little sister Annie is in her pink nightdress sitting beside me playing with her doll. Annie keeps her dolls perfect, especially Baby Fresh Doll, who is Annie's most prized possession. Baby Fresh Doll smells like baby powder.

Suddenly, I hear the faucet running at full blast and I turn to see Jackie running back and forth into the kitchen filling up a small bowl of water.

"What are you doing?" I ask her as she runs by in her silky blue Dove short-shorts and rainbow T-shirt.

Jackie doesn't answer.

"Jackie," I yell again, this time louder.

Again, no answer.

I see Jackie run by again. This time she is carrying an even bigger bowl of water.

"Jackie, answer me!" I scream. "What are you doing?"

I smell smoke, and even before I hear the siren of the alarm go off, I know there is a fire. Jackie likes playing with matches. *Oh no*, I think. *This is bad.*

"Get a towel and fan the alarm," I yell at Annie, who is sniffing at the air.

Annie is holding Baby Fresh Doll, who is wrapped in Annie's long hair. Annie throws down Baby Fresh Doll and grabs a towel from the bathroom and starts fanning the smoke alarm in the hallway. The alarm keeps blaring like a siren. *Shit*, I think. *The neighbors will hear.* Dad's friend Gene lives next door.

I race into the living room and see tall flames the color of Ronald McDonald's hair. *That is a lot of fire*, I think. The whole place could burn down, like Tara.

Jackie is throwing the water from her bowl on the curtains, the ones Mom bought from Montgomery Ward after saving for months.

Next to the drapes is our favorite chair. We call it the King Chair because it looks like a throne of black velvet. The King Chair is also on fire. I see it smoking and can smell the charred velvet. Racing out the front door, I turn on the spout and grab the green water hose and run back into the living room. I aim the hose at the curtains and at the King Chair, but there is no water. The hose is twisted.

Jackie is looking at the flames like she is frozen. "Jackie," I scream at her. "Wonder Twin, straighten out the hose. Please! Mom will kill us if we burn down the house!"

Jackie starts as if I woke her up and runs to the hose and starts untwisting.

"Wonder Twin powers, activate, form of a waterfall," she yells.

I aim the hose. A thick stream of water hits the walls, curtains, and King Chair. The flames go out with a whoosh.

We fist-bump and Jackie sighs and says, "Whew. That was close."

Annie walks into the living room. She looks at Jackie and whines, "You killed the King Chair, Wacky Jackie! I can't believe you killed the King Chair."

Jackie shrugs her shoulders and says, "Yeah, who cares, Anna Banana. Fuck it."

"Yeah, Annie, a lot of help you were. You just stood there," I say and pull her ponytail.

Annie motions at the door, "Mom is getting home soon. You're in trouble, make that a double."

I look at her and scowl. "Annie, you better not say anything or we will hurt Baby Fresh Doll. Now help us clean this up."

Annie nods in agreement.

We all work for hours doing our best to clean up the mess, but there is just no way to hide it. The carpet is soaked, the drapes are black at the edges, and the King Chair is burnt. The wall behind the King Chair is dark gray.

We hear Mom's key in the lock. Jackie and I run to our room. Annie stays by the living room.

About a minute later, we hear Annie say to Mom, "Mommy, Mommy, you won't believe what happened, Jackie almost burned the living room down."

Jackie and I look at each other and wait for it.

"What?" Mom screams. Then we hear Mom moaning, "Oh my god. My beautiful curtains. My gorgeous King Chair." Mom keeps saying it over and over like she can't believe it.

Annie starts tattling some more. "The twins had to grab the hose. Jenny got the fire out. The fire alarm was so loud, it hurt my ears. Baby Fresh started crying because we were scared."

When Mom walks into our room, she is quiet. Her eyes get dark and she starts muttering to herself. Jackie and I are sitting on my bed together holding hands.

"Come here," Mom tells Jackie and leads her into the kitchen. I follow. Mom takes out a book of matches like she is going to burn the tips of Jackie's fingers with a match. Jackie just scrunches up her face but does not cry. I can't watch and look down. My stomach hurts and tears well up in my eyes and I say, "Mom, please stop." Mom looks at me and throws them away. The ache in my stomach eases. I know Mom feels bad now. Mom hugs us both. She looks so tired and sad.

"Wait till your dad sees the mess," Mom sighs.

We don't tell Dad the story because he gets home from work after eight and you can smell the beer on his breath and hear the slur in his words. Dad doesn't even notice the mess in the living room until that weekend.

That same night, I walk into Jackie's room with my dog-eared copy of *Gone with the Wind*. She has her head in her arms. I tap her arm and say, "Here, Wonder Twin, you can read my favorite book. There's a fire scene in here, too."

"Ha, Jenny," Jackie says, looking at me with a grimace. Her eyes are watery.

She puts the book under her pillow with a smile and says with a snort, "Don't think you'll get it back."

The Plastic Cheese

Our house in Ontario is the color of dirt. Large bushes stand in front of the two windows that face the street. The yard needs to be mowed.

Inside, Mom is screaming again. I made the mistake of being a smart aleck by mimicking Mom pulling her hair as she yells Dad's name, and she saw me doing it. She has gone ballistic, which means crazy. She has that look in her eyes that means *Run*.

Dad is late getting home from work again and that's why Mom is having a fit. Dad likes to stop and get a beer at the bar down the street with Johnny R, a guy he works with. Johnny R has red hair and freckles and looks like Richie Cunningham from "Happy Days." We call him Johnny R because he has the same first name as Dad.

Mom says Dad likes hanging out with low-life losers. Mom says that only white trash go to the bar every night after work. I think Dad's just tired after moving furniture and wants to have fun. Dad loves to joke around, and when he laughs he pats his belly and slaps his knees. Sometimes, he even wiggles his false teeth. Dad works for the Mayflower moving company and drives a large green-and-yellow truck with a ship on the side. He gets a lot of stuff for free.

But poor Mom always has to chase Dad down. All Mom wants is for him not to drink so much. She says she just wants him at home where he belongs. "Damn cowboys," she mutters. "They're always wandering."

Before Mom can throw anything, I race out the sliding-glass back door and run to the park down the street. Jackie and Annie are in their bedrooms, but I can't wait for them. I keep turning my head to look back to see if they're coming while I run to the park.

Sometimes, when I look at Mom's face, I don't recognize her. When she's mad, it's as if something snaps in her. I call that person Bad Mom. I like Nice Mom, who is my real mom. Nice Mom takes me to the library and lets me buy all the books I want from the thrift store. Nice Mom makes me Kraft macaroni and cheese and mashed potatoes from the box even though Dad says we need to eat homemade food like his beef roast and gray vegetables.

The park is a quick walk, only a couple of blocks away from our house on the corner of Glenn and D Street. It is Saturday and it is only eight in the morning. The park is empty, and I sit in what I call the Plastic Cheese. It is a maze made out of concrete and has holes in it like Swiss cheese. It looks like a castle. The Plastic Cheese stands about five feet high and smells metallic inside, like stale piss and medicine mixed together.

I sit inside and start thinking. Why do Mom and Dad fight so much? Do they hate each other? Mom says it's because Dad is always drinking and Dad says it's because

Mom is always complaining. The cops sometimes come to our house because of the fights. Mom says the noisy asshole neighbors keep calling the cops because they have nothing better to do. The neighbor kids make fun of us, especially Chris, who lives down the street. He's a few years older than us.

Yesterday, Jackie and I were walking by Chris' house and he was standing in his front yard.

Chris looked and us and said with a smirk, "Your mom hates you. That's why she's always yelling and cussing." Chris said it like it was funny. I knew it wasn't true, the part about her hating us, but, well, she does yell and curse a lot. Despite myself, my eyes watered up.

I shook my head and looked at Jackie, who ran up and pushed Chris to the ground and told him to take it back. Chris ran into his house like a scared little baby. "Serves him right," Jackie said. "He's a shithead and a wimp."

"Good job," I chirped back with a smile.

"Wonder Twin powers, activate," Jackie said in our usual singsong way with a fist-bump.

"Form of a kick-ass," I said with a wave of my arm and a kick of my leg in the air like Bruce Lee in the kung fu movies Dad makes us watch.

At the park, I snap back to the present. I start reading where I left off in my favorite book, *Gone with the Wind*. Scarlett is a spoiled brat. Mom would slap her silly if she was her daughter. Dad got me the hardcover book from someone when he was moving their house. He also found me a bunch of Nancy Drew mysteries for free. I can't wait to read them. There's one about a clock that I read before and it is super creepy.

In my Plastic Cheese, I turn a page and think about how Scarlett had to leave Tara behind. I think to myself, I need to get out of here too. "One day," I whisper.

Could I leave Annie and Jackie behind? I bet they're in their rooms. Mom is probably screaming at them to get up. Annie will be fine because she is the baby and hides under the bed. She never gets hit. Neither do I because I have my act down to a science. Even if it doesn't hurt at all, and Mom's punches rarely hurt much, I cry and scream like a banshee.

Jackie is the one who makes Mom see red because Jackie won't cry. Jackie gets this look on her face while she's getting hit—it's hard to describe, like she's not home, like a vacant house or a lonely tree. Whenever Jackie gets hit, I beg Mom, "Please, Mom, stop. Please stop!" It sometimes works. I have taken a slap or two for my efforts. I know Jackie appreciates it.

I sit in the Plastic Cheese and think of Jackie and Annie. Will they be OK without me there? I have to get home.

I run.

My Frog Shirt

I am wearing my green frog T-shirt. I wear it at least two days out of the week. It brings me good luck. For some reason, whenever I am wearing it, the house is calm. I am also a voracious reader. That means I read a lot. Mom calls me a bookworm and I sometimes read a book a day. I love happy endings.

I read super quick, which is useful, but it can cause problems when my teacher doesn't believe I am finished reading a paragraph. Sometimes, I even have to pretend to be reading long after I'm finished so my teacher doesn't question me. My sisters and I are all in GATE. I know the GAT stands for *gifted and talented*. I don't know what the E stands for.

We don't speak Spanish. I think it's because the tios call Dad names in Spanish and make fun of him. Mom has a lot of brothers and they all live in Orange County. Uncle Roland is my favorite. He is my godfather, and he drives a big van that has a swirl of palm trees painted on each side. Roland has a big beard, wears shiny sunglasses, and looks and sounds just like Wolfman Jack, the famous deejay on the radio. Whenever the tios see Dad they whisper and laugh and yell, "Hola, gordito." Sometimes, they will call him borracho if he's drinking. I always scowl at them to try to get them to stop. Poor Dad, that's why he hates family reunions and gets drunk.

Mom always tells us that her brothers said she should not marry a gringo, but that she always liked cowboys. "Cowboys are romantic," Mom says, like one of the characters in a Harlequin romance. It must be the Western shirts and the Big John belt buckle that Dad wears. When they go out, Dad wears his jeans, a Western shirt with a bolo tie, his shit-kicking boots, and a big cowboy hat. Mom wears a dark blue-jean cowboy suit that has fringe. They look just like Dad's favorite country-western singers, Johnny Cash and Loretta Lynn.

I want to tell you their history. It's important to the story. As Mom tells it, she and Dad met in Oregon at a honky-tonk. A honky-tonk is a cowboy bar. There's a honky-tonk in a movie called *Urban Cowboy* with John Travolta that Dad took us to see a couple months ago. It has that song with the fiddle in it called "The Devil Went Down to Georgia." Dad loves that song. He has it on eight-track.

Mom says she was the only Mexican in that honky-tonk. She says many of the white people had never seen someone brown before other than the Indians from the reservations. Dad told Mom he had never met a Mexican. After Mom and Dad started talking, Mom says that they got along really well. Mom says she knew Dad was the one. She liked his blue eyes. Dad asked Mom out and offered to make her a chicken in a can. Mom says that chicken in a can was kind of like a baked ham in a can.

Mom had moved to Oregon from Orange County because she was trying to get her son David into a deaf school. Oregon had one of the best deaf schools in the United States. David was only five years old and too much for Mom to handle. Mom always says he looked like me. If you put our pictures side by side, we look like twins.

I have to piece everything together because Mom won't tell us the whole story. She only shares a little bit at a time. Mom and Dad started living together after only knowing each other for two weeks. This all happened before they were our mom and dad, but I don't know how else to talk about them. I guess I could call them John and Judy, but to me they're just Mom and Dad.

Mom explains that in those days, her moving in with Dad was risqué, which means shocking. I don't think Mom had anywhere else to go because she was working as a nanny and they fired her. Mom told me that when she told Dad she had nowhere to go, he said he would take care of her and her little boy.

The rest is like their own sad little book. One night, Dad didn't come home. Mom went looking for him and was holding David by the hand walking down the street from bar to bar. At a red light, David ran into the street and got hit by a car and he died. I can picture Mom crying in the street. I don't think Mom ever forgave herself or Dad. I think that's why their marriage is so bad—they started out with bad luck and it followed them. Maybe they're cursed.

You will not believe it, but Dad also lost a child. It's a

horrible story, like in a horror movie. One day, I asked him about the tattoo he has on his arm of a baby angel. Dad's eyes got watery and then he told me that before he met my mom, a babysitter threw his baby daughter Debbie against the wall and she died. His ex-wife Tiny never forgave him and left him. He said that is why Tiny didn't let him see the two daughters he had with Tiny who are my half-sisters, Barbara and Roberta, who are a lot older than us.

Mom and Dad work really hard. All they do is work but Dad says one day he is going to open a bar or a donut shop. That's his dream. Mom will look at Dad and say with a raised eyebrow and in a voice like she doesn't believe it will ever happen, "John, you and your dreams!"

Mom is a waitress and now she works at a Chinese restaurant that serves a kind of Chinese food called Cantonese. Before that, Mom worked at a coffee shop. Mom's work uniform is red polyester with black Asian flowers. Dad usually gets home from work at five from his job moving furniture for the Mayflower moving company. He's supposed to pick up me and my sisters at my mom's friend Mary's house on his way home. He's usually late. Sometimes, he forgets.

When Dad is late picking us up, he smells like beer and will drive us home in his pickup swerving the whole way home. Mary's daughters, Melinda and Pamela, are our best friends. Mom always tries to pay Mary for watching us after school every day, but Mary won't take money and always says, "No, Judy. No quiero dinero."

Occasionally, Mary lets Mom bring her some takeout from the restaurant. Mary's husband Arturo loves the

Chinese duck. Mom sometimes brings us home orange almond cookies in a big plastic bag. They are the broken ones, but they still taste delicious. Sitting in my frog shirt, reading my book, I eat them with a big glass of milk, dreaming of writing my own stories.

Broken Cookies

Mom used to bring us broken almond cookies
from the Chinese restaurant she worked at.
The cookies came in a clear plastic bag.
"These are the cast-offs," she would say.
Us girls would howl with delight,
stuffing our faces with the sweet mess.

Mom would snap at us in an angry voice.
She would scream, yell, and hit,
after a night of bringing people their almond chicken
and weighing down her arms with plates.
She remembers the white customer who
called her a Mexican,
snapped his fingers, and asked her if she spoke English.

"Who the hell do you think you are?" Mom says.
"I was born here and married a white man.
I speak better English than you."
"I should have told the gringo to
shove his tip up his ass," she says later.
She always had confidence that way.

Like when the security guy stopped us
at the Kmart when we were little.
"Your jeans look too new," he said.
Mom flipped the guy off

and shouted at him,
"They don't make jeans this pretty here."

The jeans were dark blue with white stitching.
With roller skates drawn on the back, and
real shoelaces dangling from the back pockets.
How hard she worked for us.
Back then, my sisters and I never understood
how much she had to put up with.

I crave those almond cookies.
I buy them from the 99-cent store,
I break the cookies into pieces,
remembering and thinking,
She really did love us.
She really did.

Banana Bikes and Fur Coats

We skipped third grade, so we're in fourth grade now. Mom says I'm the oldest because I'm nine minutes older than Jackie. People can't seem to tell us apart. I don't think we look alike even though we have the same tan skin and brown, frizzy hair. Jackie has always been bigger than me. I wear a size eight or ten in jeans, but Jackie wears a size twelve. Mom calls her hefty and says I am skinny. Our younger sister Annie is sixteen months younger than us twins. Mom says that when we were all babies, it was almost like having triplets. Annie is a bit on the round side, too. Her dark, pin-straight hair falls just above her butt. She has light skin, more like Dad's side of the family.

Sometimes, people think Annie's all white. Just last week, we were walking to school on our usual route down D Street. Jackie was pulling on Annie's scarf while I kept tripping and pushing her. We were about halfway to school when an old, gray-haired white lady came out of her apartment and yelled, "You damn Mexicans, leave that little white girl alone!" Jackie flipped the lady off. Together we screamed, "Shut up, you old witch! She's not white, she's Mexican and she's our sister!"

Afterward, Jackie and I fist-bumped. "Wonder Twin powers, activate! Form of badasses!" we said. The next day on the way to school, I picked one of the white wicked witch's roses and plucked off the petals on the sidewalk.

Annie is my mother's favorite. She can do no wrong.

And, even worse, Annie always gets the best gifts because there is only one of her and two of us twins. Everything has to match for us twins. People even call us the banana-bike twins because Mom bought Jackie and me matching bright yellow bicycles. Annie has a candy-apple-red bicycle. Mom says it was because there was only one red bike left. I don't believe it.

Whenever I ride my bike, I get mad. Yes, I know I should be grateful, that there are starving kids everywhere like Mom says, and all that. But I'm not grateful for my banana bike when Annie rides by me on her apple-red bike ringing her bell to spite me. The ringing bell stays in my ears. Annie's bike is so shiny and beautiful. I want to cry. Whenever I look at my bike, I think *Stupid yellow banana bike*.

Today, Jackie and I decided to fix it. Mom and Annie were at the store. We waved goodbye. "Grab her bike," I whispered to Jackie as they drove away. Jackie walked Annie's red bike as we skipped to the park. When we got there, we took turns ramming it into trees. I grabbed dirt and spread it over the bike's bright white seat and added water from the fountain until her seat was covered with mud. We laughed so hard I almost peed my pants.

"Wait until Annie sees her bike all messed up," Jackie cackled. We huddled together giggling. "She will cry like the little baby she is," I said. "Yeah," Jackie said as she wrinkled her face like a baby crying. "Waaaaaaa!"

A couple of hours later, Annie came home with Mom and the minute she saw her bike she started whimpering. "My bike is ruined, it's ruined." Tears ran down her little face and she wiped at her runny nose with her mitten-covered hand.

I felt a twinge of regret in my stomach until Annie whined, "Mommy, my red bike is ugly now," and I thought of my yellow banana bike and felt glad. Mom slapped at me, screamed, then chased after Jackie with a broom. But it was worth it, even though Mom bought Annie a new seat and a pretty basket that weekend.

But that's not the worst thing we ever did to Annie.

We were seven and Annie was five. One winter day, Mom called us into the living room. She was still wearing her waitressing uniform and her big, ugly shoes.

"These are fancy and very expensive," Mom said as she smiled wide and placed a white plastic bag with a Kmart logo in front of each one of us girls. Mom's eyes shined. Mom was like that. One minute she would be crazy and screaming and the next minute she would do something super nice like spend all of her tips on a present for us.

Annie opened her bag first and out came a beautiful snowy fur coat, pure white with pink lining. Annie put on the white coat and she looked like a snow-white rabbit princess. "So cute!" I said jumping up and down. Jackie was clapping. This was one of the best days ever.

Next, Jackie and I opened our bags at the same time and pulled out light brown fur jackets with dark brown lining. Jackie and I looked at each other, reading each other's minds. Jackie's eyes frowned and she could see my disappointment.

Brown fur coats.

"Do you like them?" Mom asked.

"I love my jacket!" I said with fabricated glee. I knew I

should have been grateful, but I couldn't stop staring at Annie as she preened and pranced in her white coat with the hint of pink lining peeking out. She looked just like a snow bunny.

"I would have got you all white ones," Mom said, "but there was only one white one left. The brown ones are still pretty, aren't they?" Yes, they were, but still Annie's jacket was prettier.

I looked at Mom and said, "Yes, Mom, I love my coat; it's beautiful," running my hand down the soft arm of the coat. It was soft and cute, but not like Annie's. I wanted the white coat with the pink lining more than anything. I wanted to be a snow bunny, plain and simple. Snow bunnies were not brown.

Jackie put on her coat, but it was too tight and as she pulled the sides of the coat together trying to zip it, Mom pulled her arm and said, "Don't try and zip it, I'll take it back tomorrow and get you a bigger size." Jackie grimaced.

That night, talking in whispers by the glow of our nightlight, I hatched a plan with Jackie. We couldn't help ourselves. The next day, going to school, I walked with Annie up Glenn Street and made a turn on D Street as always. Jackie walked slowly behind us. As we rounded the corner, I turned and gave a wink. Jackie ran up and pushed Annie into a puddle of water and mud. Her formerly alabaster coat would never be pure as snow ever again. She was brown now, just like us.

Nancy Drew and Me

My room is small and messy. One of my favorite songs is "Taxi Dancer" by Shaun Cassidy. The song is playing on my record player as I sprawl out on my shiny purple bedspread, the one Mom bought for me at Kmart. I have a poster of Wonder Woman tacked up on my wall and when I'm bored, I imagine myself throwing my lasso around people, flipping my shiny hair, and raising my gold bracelets to ward off bullets. I wish my name was Lynda like the actress who plays Wonder Woman.

Mom hates that I have clothes stuffed under the bed. Books are piled on the floor. There are Laura Ingalls Wilder's *Little House on the Prairie* books mixed with Judy Blume paperbacks and S.E. Hinton novels. Mom loves to read just like I do. She calls it her escape. She loves romance novels and *True Story* magazine. Some of my books are from the library and I bought some from the Scholastic catalogue. Mom gives us the change from the tips she gets at the Chinese restaurant to buy books. Mom is many things, angry and crazy being two of them, and hardworking and generous being another two. She is what some might call a contradiction.

"Read as many books as you can," Mom always says. "That way you won't have to wait tables like me."

We have a routine. On Saturday mornings, before her shift at the restaurant, Mom takes us to the Ontario library, which is next door to her work. Jackie, Annie, and I always check out the maximum number of books allowed. I try not to drop them in the bathtub. More often than not, my allowance goes to pay the late fees. Jackie likes *The Wizard of Oz* books, and fairy tales, which I like, too. I love *The Hobbit* and have read it twice. Mom is patient with us at the library. She lets us browse. If I could, I would live in the library and burrow in the stacks.

Annie always gets little-kid books, and I make her check some out for me so I can get more books. Annie is not as advanced in reading as we are. Right now, I am reading all of the Nancy Drew and Hardy Boys books, and I found an author called Fitzgerald that I like in the adult section. He writes about rich people mostly.

Mom walks by my doorway in her red uniform with the black accents. The closures are wound-up little spools. Dad calls it her Oriental uniform.

"Clean up this damn room, Jenny," Mom says. Something is brewing. Mom is like two different characters. If this were a fairy tale, she would play both roles, the wicked stepmother and the fairy godmother.

"OK, Mom," I say and nod my head at her. I squirrel under the covers with my Nancy Drew mystery. It is peaceful and I am falling into the book, like into a well of water. I'm immersed. It is quiet. No one is fighting, for once. Annie and Jackie are at Melinda and Pam's house. I am staying home from school today because I played sick.

I hear Mom calling Mary to see if Dad has picked up my sisters. He is late coming home again. Mom is mad. Her voice is getting higher and higher. It's not a mystery. You don't have to be Nancy Drew to figure out her moods. She's easy to figure out. Mom paces by my door, cursing and muttering to herself. I hear her say, "Damn. He's probably with those losers at the bar."

I put the covers over my head. Maybe if I'm quiet, Mom will forget that I'm here. I don't want her to start screaming at me. I know how fast her anger can flame up and don't want it directed at me. I've learned the hard way that it is best to take the path of least resistance with Mom. Whenever Jackie argues with her, it never goes well. Jackie has the battle scars to prove it.

I don't know why Dad just can't come home after work on time. That's all Mom wants. She tells him, "John, dammit, is it too much to ask for you to come home instead of going to the bar after work?" Dad just shakes his head at her and says, "Judy, you can take the cowboy out of the bar, but you can't take the bar out of the cowboy."

Dad loves bars. He wants to own his own bar one day. Whenever Dad's late, I picture him sitting on a stool, waving his glass in the air, laughing with his friends in his green Mayflower uniform. The other part of me thinks Mom should just relax because Dad always comes home. Yes, he's always late, but he always comes home. He is always there on a Saturday morning to make us pancakes with jelly inside and eggs with bacon so crispy that it breaks into pieces.

I love watching Dad making his pancakes. He always says, "You gotta wait till the bubbles pop, Jenny." Dad stands there with his spatula while I count the bubbles popping, and then when they're all popped I'll yell out "Go!" and Dad will flip the pancake. When he's flipped all of the pancakes, Dad screams out in his jolly breakfast baritone, "Time for breakfast, girls!"

Dad's other favorite things, other than cooking and drinking, are card games. He taught us cards when we were really little. During the first lesson, Jackie and I nodded along, but Annie looked confused. Annie patted my leg and raised her hands in confusion. I said to her in a whisper, "I'll explain it later."

"First you deal each player seven cards," Dad said, shuffling the cards sideways, pushing his false teeth out and crossing his eyes. "Jokers are worth fifty points, aces are worth twenty, and anything eight and above is ten points and anything below eight is worth five points."

Dad continued on slowly, "OK, girls, now let's just try and play a practice game. The first person I deal to gets eight cards and they have to discard one."

Annie had all her cards bunched up together. Dad took them from her and made them into a fan, taking her cards out and putting them in order. Dad was patient. "Try and group your cards together," he explained, "so you can play them. Aces with aces, cards of the same suit in sequence."

We usually play with one deck but sometimes with two. Dad taught us how to do a dealer shuffle, and I practice for hours, putting my thumbs under the cards after each shuffle so that it creates a waterfall of cards that click against one another. We started off playing 500-point games on Friday nights when Mom worked late. But 500-point games would only last a night, so eventually we started playing 5,000-point games that would take many nights of cards to finish.

Dad takes his rummy very seriously and always puts his hand on his chin and squints his eyes to look at the cards in his hand. "C'mon, Dad, hurry," I always plead. When one of us lays down a card in the discard pile that is "playable," Dad shouts "Rummy" and slams his hand down on the card. Dad gloats and plays cards with us like we are adults, except we have no money to bet. Jackie and I always say, "When it comes to rummy, Dad has no mercy."

I snap back to now. I hear Mom yelling into the phone. My shoulders tense up and I jump up from the bed. Mom stomps into my bedroom, shaking her head, and bellows, "I am going to pick up your sisters and go find your lowlife dad."

Mom storms out and I hear the door slam. I sigh with relief. I am right in the middle of the book. In this one, Nancy is trying to find out the mystery of the hidden window. When I was really little, I dressed up as Nancy Drew for the Ontario Library Book Parade after Annie stole my Laura Ingalls Wilder prairie-girl idea which was a bunch of bullshit. To make it worse, Mom bought Annie a bonnet just like the one Laura Ingalls Wilder used to wear.

Nancy Drew was less recognizable but, on the cool scale, I told Annie with a smirk that Nancy Drew could kick Laura Ingalls' ass any day. For my costume, I wore a turtleneck and a short skirt with tights. Just to make sure everyone knew who I was, I carried a spyglass and a sign that said, "I'm Nancy Drew." Everyone really dug my costume. I told Annie she looked old and dusty.

The thing I like best about the Nancy Drew books is that they all start out in the same way.

In every book, Nancy gets a new case and has an adventure. She ends up solving many mysteries in each book. Nancy is motherless, but a housekeeper named Hannah lives with Nancy and her dad and acts like a mom should. Moms should be nice—at least I think so. They should act like Carol on "The Brady Bunch." Carol never screams at her kids. She never, ever hits them. She never calls her kids names when she is mad at Mr. Brady. Nice moms talk about nice things in soft voices. In the Brady Bunch house, no one throws food at each other at the dinner table like my mom and dad do, at least not in an angry way, only in a fun, food-fight way.

The house is quiet. I am wrapped up in my book. When I love a book, I get transported and, right now, I feel as if I am Nancy Drew. In the end, as I knew she would, Nancy solves the case and gets her reward. With the turning of the last page, I hear a door slam and Annie and Jackie come running into my room.

"Dad's drunk," Annie whispers, her long brown ponytail swinging. What's she worried about? No matter how mad Mom gets, Annie never gets hit. Jackie walks in a second later and sits on my bed. "Hey, sicko," she jokes. "Better get dressed before the fireworks start and we have to walk to the park. Unless you want to walk there in your Wonder Woman Underoos."

"But it's getting dark," Annie whines. "And cold...."

"Shut up, Annie," Jackie says, and socks her in the arm. Annie starts kicking her.

"Stop fighting, you two," I order in my oldest-sister voice.

Minutes later, I hear glass breaking and Mom and Dad screaming at each other. I grab a book off the floor and put my flashlight in my pocket.

Jackie and I look at each other and I grab Annie's hand. Time to go. Our own adventure is just beginning.

Summertime

It's near the end of summer. Dad's tattered blue pickup truck with an equally tattered camper shell sits in the driveway along with Mom's new small brown Pinto station wagon. Loud yells and screams are coming from inside the house.

We can hear glass breaking, a door slamming. We watch from up on the roof.

Mom rushes out of the house dragging Annie by the hand. Annie is crying, fat tears running down her face, her long brown hair disheveled. "I don't want to go by myself," she sobs.

Dad comes outside; his white skin is sunburned bright red. His ample stomach bulges out of the bottom of his green Mayflower uniform.

"Judy, get back here, don't leave," he pleads.

"No, fuck you, John, I'm leaving you! You son of a bitch! Keep those twins, they're little bitches. I'll take Annie," Mom yells back.

We stare at the chaotic, familiar scene below. It is almost like a dysfunctional version of the sitcoms we watch so obsessively on TV.

Mom pushes Annie into the back seat screaming, "Stop crying." Mom starts the car, and Dad runs to the car and bangs on the window begging her not to leave. Mom flips him off and drives away.

Annie cranes her head out the window and looks up at us on the roof. I wave.

Watching Mom and Annie drive away, I feel as if I swallowed a grapefruit whole. All of the bad things that could happen run through my mind like a movie.

Mom could run a red light and get hit by a semi, or she could hit the center divider on the freeway and get them pinned and trapped inside the car. Or, maybe, she could drive away and never come back? I shake my head to make the thoughts go away, and count to myself in multiples of five. That always calms me down.

Dad shakes his head and shouts into the sky, "Girls, where are you?" Slowly, I scoot down the slanted roof on my behind and go backwards down the ladder to the ground. Jackie is right behind me. Dad comes into the backyard and gives me a hug, which I try and squirm out of. "Let's go get pizza," Dad says with a smile, but his eyes stay sad. Jackie pats his shoulder as we walk inside the house to change.

When we get to the Pizza Hut, Dad orders a medium pepperoni pizza, a pitcher of root beer, and a pitcher of Budweiser. Dad feeds the small black-and-white TV carefully with four quarters. Each quarter is fifteen minutes of TV time. We watch "Different Strokes" then "The Facts of Life." Dad grumbles that he would rather be watching "MASH."

Jackie and I gulp down glass after glass of root beer as Dad downs glass after glass of beer. I put a piece of pizza on his plate and say, "Hurry and eat, Dad, before Jackie eats it all." Jackie punches my arm. We fight over the last slice of pizza and I finally give in. Jackie stuffs the last piece of pizza in her mouth. As cheese and sauce dribbles down her chin, she says, "Annie is going to be mad she missed this."

Laughing, I get up to go to the bathroom. In the bathroom, when I am done peeing, I flush the toilet and think, "If I can finish counting to ten before the flushing stops, then they're OK." I finish counting right before the flushing stops. "God, if you're there, please make sure they're OK," I whisper, crossing myself. Later, I will make myself throw up the pizza.

I walk slowly back to the red-and-white checkered table and see Jackie prodding Dad awake, saying, "C'mon Dad, time to go." The beer pitcher is empty. We climb into the back of Dad's pickup shell and lay down, our heads on green packing blankets. The truck swerves a bit as we turn down Grove Avenue, and Dad sings along to "Elvira" by the Oak Ridge Boys. I love that song, especially the part with the deep-voice guy.

The radio shuts off and it's too quiet, so I poke my head through the cab to check on Dad. At the stoplight by the baseball park he starts crying. "Your Mom is crazy, but I can't leave."

"It's OK, Dad. When we get home, she'll be calm," I say.

Later that night, I sit in my bed reading. Jackie is asleep in the bed next to mine, her blue-and-white striped Kmart comforter tucked under her chin. She's drooling onto her pillow. We share a room because Jackie is afraid to sleep alone. Dad built our beds into the wall and painted them both a chalky white color even though I wanted mine painted mint green. Jackie is scared of the dark and she likes to sleep with the lights on. I always turn out the lights as soon as she falls asleep, making sure that our Wonder Woman night-light is plugged in the socket next to her bed. Annie has her own room next door, which she keeps padlocked so that we won't touch her stuff and break it.

As soon as we got home, Dad passed out on his powder blue La-Z-Boy recliner. The chair smells like his sweat. I can hear Dad snoring from the living room. I hear the key turning in the front door and Mom saying, "Wake up John, wake up, it's late. You smell like beer, go to bed." Rubbing my eyes, I hear Mom help him up.

As they pass my bedroom, I hear a thump and Mom yells, "Dammit, John! You almost broke him!"

Darn it. Dad must have bumped into the two-foot plaster Jesus that sits in the hallway. Even though I know God wouldn't like it, I wish Dad had broken the statue. Whenever I walk past Plaster Jesus in the hallway, his eyes seem to follow me, as if he is going to reach out his stigmata-covered palm and touch me. Sometimes, the statue speaks to me in my dreams. I can never remember what Plaster Jesus says.

A few minutes later, Annie inches opens the door and pads into my room, holding her Baby Fresh doll.

"Jenny, are you awake?" she whispers. I lift my head from my prayers and pat the bed beside me. Annie talks in her baby voice, "Mom took me to get hot chocolate on the way back from Uncle's house." She blows her hot-chocolate-tinged breath on me.

I breathe a sigh of relief.

The Doll Under Glass

(In my mom's voice)

Robin took the day off. Busboy out sick. They're all fucking looking at me, wanting to be waited on. Old Joe raises his hand at me, "Can I order?"

I shake my head at him, wave his hand away. Asshole. Who does he think he is?

"You're gonna have to wait for Mary to come on," I tell him.

Five minutes. Fuck, it's almost five o'clock. I am supposed to be off already.

The kids are alone in the house probably tearing it apart. Yesterday, Jackie broke the side window, the one right next to the front door. Can you believe it? She threw a rock right through it after Jenny and Annie locked her outside. I came home and there was broken glass all over the carpet. It makes me livid just to think about it.

No respect at all. I work hard. The man who runs the glass shop will charge me fifty dollars to fix the window. That's more than I make a night in tips.

At first, the twins told me a burglar did it. Their dad might have believed that shit, but not me. I am no fool. They broke my new glass table as well. They break everything. Twins are double trouble. Taught the twins to read when they were barely three and they were reading full books by four. I always knew they were special, GATE kids. Had them tested.

God gave them to me for a reason. I took those fertility drugs, prayed every night for God to give me girls. Not to replace David. Nothing could replace my first son. Just needed something to help me forget his eyes that night when he died on the stormy street. I love all my girls so very much. I would do anything for them. My twins, and little Annie, my miracle daughters.

Jenny's face is a replica of David's. Annie looks like my mother. Jackie looks just like her dad to me. Teacher says that the twins are at advanced reading level. I did that for them, not John. He was at a bar. Always at some bar, hanging out with lowlifes, drinking and gambling all our money away.

When I saw the broken window and the glass, I knew who had done it. Annie scampered off to her room. I grabbed Jackie by her arm. She didn't even try to deny it. Just looked at me. I got madder and madder. "You are fucking ungrateful," I heard myself tell her.

My head felt like it was splitting open and the next thing I remember is Jenny crying. She's always getting in my way. Jenny cried and said it was her and Annie's fault for locking Jackie out. "Just don't hit Jackie," she cried.

Later that night, John came home, beer on his breath. He swayed through the front door, his Mayflower uniform stained with sweat. He tried to make me apologize to Jackie but I told him, "Look at the fucking window. Is she going to pay for it? Are you?"

He is always taking her side. He should take her and Jenny if he loves them so much. That kid, so damn stubborn, just like John. Like father, like daughter. John's little baby.

Jackie reminds him of Barbara, that's why. Barbara—all those kids, no money, and she doesn't work.

Barbara is not my daughter, she's Tiny's daughter, and they have been divorced for years. John wants to save her. I tell him Tiny already messed that kid up, leave it alone.

Where is Gary? He is supposed to manage the restaurant, he should help me bus. His mom Edna would shit bricks if she knew how he's never around. I walk into the kitchen and grab a bus tray. At each empty table I throw the dishes inside as fast as possible. They clack together. Gotta get home. John better be home. Better not come home drunk from the bar. The gravy from the almond chicken sloshes onto my shirt. Yangtze's kitchen is so hot; I am sweating like a marrano.

"Goddamn it!"

"Judy, are you muttering to yourself again?" *Gary says in his sarcastic voice. What an asshole.*

"Yeah, yeah, yeah, Gary."

As I drive home a black cloud is settling over me. John's truck is not in the driveway.

The front door is wide open. Goddamn kids. As I shut the door, I see Annie and Jenny standing upright looking like they have a mouse under their shirts. Jenny is holding her book by her side.

"Did you guys do your chores?" *I ask.*

"Yeah, mom," *Jenny says.* "Annie vacuumed. I did the dishes."

Jackie walks into the room. She has her dad's same swagger. What is she hiding? I look around. My head is pounding, there's a haze.

"You tired, Mom?" *Jenny asks in her placating voice. The one she uses when she knows I am in a bad mood. She pats my arm and I pull away.*

"Yes, I'm tired," *I say abruptly.* "Where's your dad?"

"Not here, obviously," Jackie says nudging Jenny in her side. I see Jenny look at her with a quick head turn and elbow her. "He should be home soon," she says.

Annie says so soft that I almost can't hear her, "Mom, the china doll's house broke."

I glare at the hutch. The china doll John gave me is gone. Annie tells me with one glance. I look past the recliner and see that my doll is all alone on the coffee table with no glass dome over her. Her hands have been moved, her kimono is all astray. Glass is scattered on the carpet.

Jenny and Jackie bolt for the back door. I start going through the hutch throwing things, not even knowing what I am doing. Out of the corner of my eye, I see Annie's feet shuffling toward the back door. Just like them.

"Go with your fucking sisters. Get out of here. Leave."

Annie stands still like a statue. A little doll in purple Dove shorts and a pink T-shirt, her long brown hair pulled back neatly in a ponytail.

"Now!" I scream.

I see Jackie and Jenny poke their heads around the slider. They are still here. Jenny motions toward Annie and their six small, tanned legs sprint away from view.

I throw John's favorite beer stein against the wall, the one with the mountains in the background. Blue porcelain litters the ground. Such a mess. Girls should clean it up.

Bet you I find that asshole sitting on his favorite barstool.

I get in my car and drive. As I pass John Galvin Park, I see Annie on the swings. Jackie is pushing her. I make sure Jenny is sitting in the Plastic Cheese, as usual. It's OK.

The girls are fine. I'll be right back.

My Tia Tilly

Mom took us out of school today so that we could go with her to visit our Aunt Tilly. Tilly is married to Mom's brother.

Mom does this every so often because she hates driving to Orange County by herself. We don't mind missing school.

Annie grabbed shotgun, so Jackie and I are stuck in the back seat together. We make faces at people through the dusty windows of the Pinto. Jackie occasionally flips people off and I elbow her in the side, trying to get her to stop. I catch Mom's stare in the rearview mirror as she screams, "Fucking cut it out, twins!" We know to stop or else risk her reaching backwards to slap at us from the front seat.

Even when we are not goofing off, driving with Mom is always dangerous. She drives erratically, telling people off as she goes. "Asshole!" she'll yell and honk her horn when someone cuts her off. "Fuck a duck" is another of her favorite sayings, and we have to pinch each other to keep from laughing out loud. Mom hates semitrucks; she closes her eyes if they get too close, like right now.

"Mom!" I yell, "Be careful, the truck is...."

Mom turns around and glares me into silence before I can finish my sentence. At least her eyes are open.

"Ayyyyy," Aunt Tilly says as she opens the door to her small, three-bedroom house in Buena Park. It is covered in pink stucco and has large plastic flowers that spin in the garden. As I plop down on the plastic-covered sofa to read my book, she croons, "Hola, Juana flaca, y gordita Jackie, y una bonita Annie."

You know tias, they have to label us. Tilly has to fit us into little boxes. In her boxes, I'm the skinny bookworm ("Jenny, mija, get your head out of the book and eat something. I made some rice"). Jackie is the chubby black sheep ("Tttt-ttttt, Jackie, slow down, save some for the rest of us. Judy, you gotta watch this one, she's got John's genes") and Annie, as usual, is the perfect one ("Ohhhh, Annie, come here, sweetie, you're so pretty").

Just for the record, Tilly is crazy, but we all love her. She smokes a cigarette every five minutes. Tilly has just lit up, and I can see the smoke rising like fog from the cigarette butt she just snuffed out a minute ago. She has five Siamese cats, which sit throughout the house perched on tall, tan cat-tower scratching posts. Tilly loves her cats, especially Tabitha, the evil one, who hisses at anyone who tries to pet her. We are all scared of Tabitha. A few years later, Tabitha will bite the tip of Tilly's finger off and, as the story goes, Tilly will put the little piece of finger in a Dixie cup, cover it with ice, and take it with her to the hospital, where the doctors will sew it back on. She will keep the cat.

Tilly always wears muumuus with pink backgrounds

and purple flowers. She calls them her house dresses. With her blonde hair piled on top of her head, she looks like a poorer version of Mrs. Roper from "Three's Company." Tilly is white, but she speaks fluent Spanish and cooks delicious Mexican food. Her enchiladas and homemade tamales are the best.

Tilly has a laugh like a wild horse and a dying hyena put together. Right now, I can tell by the way Tilly is laughing that she and Mom are reliving their days growing up together.

Tilly and Mom's conversations go back and forth between Spanish and English. When they speak Spanish, they think we don't understand, but we can usually figure it out. Mom and Tilly lived down the street from each other, around the corner from Knott's Berry Farm, back when it was still a real farm. Mom always says it was a simpler time back then. Talking about the olden days makes them seem younger. They tell us how Tilly married mom's brother Poncho which made them sisters as well as friends.

Mom is hunched over the dining table, stirring her coffee, alternating sips with laughter. She's laughing so hard that I can see the back of her throat. Mom never laughs like this at home. It makes me smile to see her happy. Mom doesn't have a lot to laugh about at home, what with chasing down Dad at bars and waiting tables at the restaurant five days a week and working graveyard at Circle K two nights a week.

Mom is a different person at Aunt Tilly's house. She seems calmer and she smiles a lot. I can almost picture her and Tilly as their younger selves. They talk about how they had dirt floors back then and all the crazy stuff they used to do. Tilly would stay over the house and sneak into Poncho's room late at night.

They talk about how Mom was the only brown girl in her class. Then they talk about Mom's deaf son David, who was only five when he died after being hit by a car. Mom's eyes well up when Tilly says that when she used to babysit him for Mom, David would always act up.

"Judy, remember when he locked you out of the house and tore up all the money in your purse? That boy was crazy," Tilly laughs.

Mom gets a look in her eyes as if she is seeing his face. "I know, David was a brat sometimes, wasn't he?" and whispers, "He never even heard my voice."

The best part of our visit is when they bring out the photo albums. My sisters and I all lean over the table, peeling pictures off the sticky backing of the photo album. In Mom's sixth-grade photo, she is probably about the same age I am right now. Mom has a sharp overbite and her dark skin stands out against the whiteness of her classmates in the black-and-white class photo. Mom doesn't talk much about that time. All she will say was that it was hard not knowing how to speak English well.

Other than looking at the photo album, there is not much to do at Tilly's house. Tilly and Poncho have three kids, Queytay, Richard, and Tina. They are at school. I would rather be at school than here. It's so boring. I try to read my Harlequin romance novel that Mom let me read, but Jackie and Annie won't let me. We can't even watch good TV because Tilly likes to keep it on the Spanish channel. A fat man in a bumblebee suit is dancing on the screen right now and even though we don't understand what he's saying, my sisters and I giggle in unison.

Occasionally, the three of us will fight, like tag-team wrestling. Jackie and Annie will decide that they're going to play keep-away with my Harlequin novel, or Jackie and I will steal Annie's Baby Fresh Doll and play keep-away and watch her cry. Years ago, we drew crazy eyebrows on Annie's other baby doll, so she is scared we will make Baby Fresh look like Groucho Marx. Annie and I rarely ever gang up on Jackie. Jackie is too tough and will never back down. She makes a much better friend than an enemy.

When we leave Tilly's house, Mom takes us to Huntington Beach. It's our favorite part of going to Orange County and makes the long drive and hours of boredom at Aunt Tilly's house well worth it. I get so excited when I smell the salt in the air that I roll down the back window. Jackie and I start screaming, which causes Mom to wince. As soon as Mom parks, we jump out of the car and race to find a spot on the sand to put our bath towels. Mom lays out her blanket. Annie walks down to the water's edge to gather shells. Annie carefully washes each shell before putting it in her plastic bucket. She's just as careful with the shells as she is with her dolls. I bury Jackie in the sand, which she loves.

The waves get bigger and bigger, and Jackie jumps up and yells, "Let's swim, Wonder Twin! Form of a wave!" We speed into the water, jumping up and down with the rhythm of the surf for what seems like forever. I get water in my nose and walk toward Annie who is still collecting shells. I wave at Jackie to follow me to shallower water.

Mom is still sitting on the beach reading her *True Story* magazine. Mom hates the water more than a cat even does, maybe because she never learned how to swim. We shout, "Come in the water, Mom! C'mon!" Mom ignores us and continues reading, munching on the peanut butter and jelly crackers Tilly packed for her.

We get Annie to put down her bucket and bodysurf with us. Once we are covered in salt and sea and have sand down the backs of our swimsuits, we lay down on our beach towels to get a tan and dry off our suits. Mom shares her snacks and we all laugh together. Mom is happy.

The sun warms my skin and my eyes start to close, when without warning, Mom says, "Let's go, girls." Mom has the same scowl she always gets when she is wondering where Dad is.

I know it's time to go home, but I don't want to leave. When we get home, I know a fight will be brewing, just like it always is, and I want to stay here in the sun.

Grandpa's House

We are on our way to Grandpa's house. He lives by the cow farms in Norco. To get there, you have to take Euclid Avenue all the way south. It takes about an hour and I always get carsick from the winding road.

Annie tries to claim the front seat. She outruns me to Mom's Pinto and puts her hand on the passenger door handle. She knows the rules: Oldest always gets the front seat unless you tag and call it. I am older than my twin Jackie by nine minutes and claim my birthright. From catechism, I know the story of Cain and Abel and that being first out means something.

"You twins sit in back," Mom says.

Annie is the youngest and the most favored. *Not this time*, I think to myself.

"But, Mom, you know I get carsick, just like you do. When I sit in the back, my head spins. I could throw up," I say in a matter-of-fact voice.

Mom nods her head at me. She knows I am prone to vomiting when carsick or nervous. I had thrown up on our dentist a couple of years earlier when he tried to put a foul-smelling fluoride on my teeth. He never let Mom or me forget it.

"There she is," the dentist would say with a funny grimace whenever he saw me. "You didn't eat breakfast, did you?"

"Fine," Mom says. "Jenny, you sit in the front."

I stick my tongue out at Annie when Mom turns and gets in the car. Annie wrinkles her nose. Foiled.

On the way to Grandpa's house, Jackie and I fight as usual. Jackie keeps on kicking the back of my seat. She keeps kicking and kicking until I turn around and swat at her.

Mom glares at us. "Stop it or I will fucking pull over." When she gets mad, Mom's eyes turn dark. Jackie stops kicking.

The scenery flies by. I forgot my book at home and play with the radio. Right now, I am reading *Gone with the Wind* again. I plan on making my way through the famous authors alphabetically. When I have a favorite book, I read it over and over. Mom says all of us girls are gifted and that it comes from her side of the family.

I know we are getting close when I get a whiff of the thick smell of manure. Jackie and Annie are plugging their noses in the back seat, laughing.

"It smells like the bathroom after Dad takes a poop," Annie says.

We crack up and even Mom smiles. Mom is nicer on these trips. We get to see a different side of her. She is not stressed out or arguing with my dad about what time he got home, where he went, or who he was with. It is almost as if we get to see Mom as her best self. I never want to leave

Grandpa's house because I know that when we get home,
Nice Mom might be gone.

We pull up to Grandpa's house. His house is on about
half an acre and weeds cover the front yard. Mom mutters,
"My goddamn brothers should come out here and clean his
yard."

Mom is the only sibling who visits regularly. We come
almost every Saturday. Mom says it's because she lives the
closest. Mom's sister and all her brothers live in Orange
County.

I think we visit often because Grandpa is our only
grandparent. My dad's mom and dad passed away a long
time ago in Montana, and Mom's mother died when she was
young.

"He's the only grandpa you got so be nice to him,"
Mom says as we pull up to the house.

Dust spirals around the car as she parks the Pinto next
to the chain-link fence that surrounds the property. Grandpa
is outside waving at us when we pull up. He is over eighty
and stands on the porch stooped over and wrinkled. He
always wears a flannel. Mom pats Grandpa's shoulder.

"Hola, Poppa," Mom says in a soft, little-girl voice.

"Hola, Judy," he croaks back.

Grandpa's voice is low. He only speaks in garbled
Spanish. Mom seems to understand him perfectly. He bends
down and kisses Annie's head and says, "Bonita."

We all know that means pretty even though we don't
speak Spanish.

"It's your dad's fault you don't know Spanish," Mom
says. "Your dad told me not to teach you because that way

you couldn't make fun of him in Spanish like my brothers do."

Mom's brothers call my dad a gringo borracho, which means *drunk white man*.

"Twins, say hi to your grandpa," Mom orders.

"Hi, Grandpa," Jackie and I say in unison.

Grandpa pats our shoulders, "Hola, gemelas." Everyone in Mom's family calls us the twins.

I sit down on the couch, which is covered with a knitted blanket. The house is dusty and smells like cigarette smoke. Grandpa gets his cigarettes out of a small wooden box. It looks like a straw dispenser and when you press down on the lever a cigarette comes out. We love playing with it, and Jackie and I take turns pressing down on the lever until Mom gives us a sharp look.

Grandpa wasn't very nice to my mom when she was young. "He didn't pay me any mind after my mother died," she says. "He just threw me away." As Mom tells it, her mom was old and had diabetes, and she died when Mom was only fourteen. Mom says she was so sad that tried to throw herself in her mother's coffin at the funeral.

Mom always says how sweet and nice her mother was. When Mom talks about her mother, she gets a look on her face that I can't describe. It's the look I picture on Scarlett O'Hara's face when she talks about Tara.

Mom says that after her mother died, everything changed. Her dad put her in a convent because he had a new white girlfriend before her mother was even in the ground. Mom hated the convent. She said the nuns were mean to her and she missed her brothers and her sister Eva. Mom kept on running away until her brothers finally persuaded her dad to let her come home. After she got back, Mom went wild. Even though Grandpa treated Mom like that, she is still nice to him.

My sisters and I also like visiting Grandpa because he always gives us change from his jar to take to the store down the street to buy candy. We sit on the couch tapping our feet waiting for him to take down the jar, which he finally does.

"Mijas," Grandpa says in his garbled voice, "quieres dinero para dulce?"

I get the gist and say, "Si, Grandpa," opening my hands. He pours coins into my outstretched palms. Jackie goes second and Annie goes last. Grandpa lets the jar linger a bit over Annie's open palms and Jackie gives me a look. We know what's happening here.

I whisper in Jackie's ear, "Don't worry, we will make everything even on the way to the store." Jackie nods.

The three of us walk down Grandpa's dusty road. The liquor store is only a couple of blocks away. Annie resists pooling our coins. "It's all mine," she whines. Annie loves money. She hoards it.

"No, it's ours," I say in my oldest-child voice, as if it is fact. "Everything should be even steven. It's only fair."

Jackie chimes in, trying to convince her, "Yeah, Annie. Be fair."

Annie hesitates for a moment but knows she doesn't have much of a choice and nods her agreement.

Outside the store, I count our pooled change and we each score a little over a dollar in quarters and dimes. I buy a big bag of five-cent candies, some cotton candy, and a Coke.

Annie gets an A&W Root Beer, gum, and a Snickers. Jackie gets a Big Hunk, an ice cream and, of course, she copies me by getting a Coke. We walk back to Grandpa's house in a single-file line. The cows moo at one another at the dairy across the street. We stand in front of the dairy watching them, counting the black-and-white cows.

"How long do you think we will stay today?" Jackie asks me. "Maybe we can ask Mom to stop by the creek after."

"You ask her, Annie," I order.

Mom is making Grandpa some canned Campbell's soup when we get back. We sit in the living room and pile our candy on the table. Soon, wrappers are scattered on the floor around us. I watch as Grandpa eats his soup slowly, spoonful after spoonful. Mom doesn't hurry him. She is only patient with Grandpa. She makes a pot of coffee and sips cup after cup sitting at the table talking to Grandpa in Spanish. My sisters and I cluster together on the couch watching PBS on his little black-and-white TV. The picture is grainy. After a couple of hours, Mom gives us the sign that it's time to go by flipping off the TV.

We pile back in the car and watch Mom say goodbye to her dad. They don't hug. Mom just pats Grandpa on the shoulder again. Mom turns around to look at him in his doorway as we drive away.

"Bye, Grandpa," we shout out the windows of the Pinto. I have the front seat again.

"Bye, mijas," Grandpa gargles back.

When we turn the corner, Annie asks Mom if we can stop at the creek and she says yes. Mom is happy. She gets out of the car and sits on a rock reading her *True Story* magazine. We wade in the creek with our pants pulled up to our knees.

After a little while, as if a switch was pulled, Mom returns to her other self. "I wonder if your dad's home from the bar," she says with a twist of her head. I see the darkness returning to her eyes as dusk falls in the sky. We pile into the car.

"I don't want to go," Jackie argues.

"Get in the car now," Mom says, her voice rising.

"Just get in the car, Jackie. I'll sit with you," I plead. Jackie gives in. We pile into the back seat as Annie practically does a cartwheel into the front seat. She pumps her fist and I hear her whisper "Shotgun!"

I sleep the whole way home in the back seat.

Grandpa dies in October. I miss going to visit Grandpa. It wasn't just the candy. The candy helped, but it was the way he looked at us, like he was smiling with his eyes, and the way Mom smiled at him. She is never like that anymore.

On Halloween, Dad decorates the house with gravestones in the front yard. The gravestones make Mom cry because she says they remind her that Grandpa is gone. In his will, Grandpa leaves his house in Norco to Mom. Dad says Mom should keep the house all for herself and tries to convince her.

"Judy, your brothers and sisters hardly ever saw him. Keep the house for the girls," Dad says pointing at us.

Mom shakes her head, scowls, and says, "My brothers helped us when we moved from Montana to California, John. Remember?"

Dad nods.

Mom tells Dad that they're selling the house and that it wouldn't be right to keep all the money from its sale. Mom splits the money with her sister Eva and all of her brothers.

"Even steven," Mom says. "That's how things should be."

Later, Mom grumbles to Dad that her family took all the furniture and didn't leave much, not even Grandpa's little cigarette box.

Movie Time

We are getting ready to go to the Mission Drive-In. The four-screen theater is just off Holt and Central in Montclair, California. It doubles as a *remate*, or swap meet. On the weekends, my best friend Melinda and her dad sell used bike parts at their stall.

Tonight, we are watching a movie called *Tron*, about a guy stuck in a video game. We wanted to see something else, but Dad loves science fiction. Last weekend, he took us to see *Star Trek II: The Wrath of Khan*. It was pretty good. Ricardo Montalbán from "Fantasy Island" played the villain.

Mom never gets to go with us because she's always working. She says Saturday nights are the best night for tips and she usually works until at least ten. It's almost better without her there because that way everything goes smooth. The one time Mom did go to the drive-in with us, she got into a fight with Dad on the way there and jumped out of the car at the stoplight. Dad had to drive after Mom and beg her to get back in the car. We missed the first fifteen minutes of the movie because of her.

Dad is in the kitchen popping popcorn in a large pot.

We watch as he turns on the heat. He waits a minute and then pours in a cup of canola oil. "The trick is letting the pan get hot," Dad says, as the pot starts to sizzle. As soon as a kernel pops, he starts shaking the pot, holding down the lid with a stained rag. We can hear the kernels making fast popping sounds, and our eyes follow his hands as he dumps the popcorn into a double bag with the Stater Brothers logo on the side. As he melts down a stick of margarine, Dad looks at me and says, "This is the good stuff, Jenny" and pours the hot margarine straight from the pan into the bag. He pulls the Morton's down from the cupboard and hands it to Jackie, who shakes it over the popcorn.

Jackie grabs a piece of the freshly salted popcorn and he slaps her hand. "C'mon, Dad, let me have a little bit," Jackie pleads with him. Dad winks and fills a plastic bowl, which we all shove our hands into, grabbing as much as possible on the first grab.

Dad turns off the TV and yells, "Time to go. Grab the lawn chairs, girls." He walks outside and starts packing up his pickup truck with the required blankets. Jackie and I scramble into the back of the camper and throw our plastic lawn chairs toward the back of the truck.

Annie climbs into the passenger seat, struggling with the Styrofoam ice chest filled with a six-pack of Shasta orange cola and a six-pack of Budweiser. "Give me that," Dad says as he takes the cooler from her hands and places it in the middle of his wide bench seat. Before starting the truck, he pulls a beer out and puts it into a green foam sleeve for the drive. He's already had a couple.

As he starts up the truck, Dad turns his head toward

us and says with a wink, "OK, girls, duck down under the packing blankets when we get there."

"Dad, put it on KISS-FM," Jackie says, poking her head through the window of the cab. Dad makes a face as he pops Loretta Lynn out of his eight-track player. "Our Lips Are Sealed" comes on the radio and we start singing along in unison.

"I'm Belinda," I tell Jackie, grabbing my hairbrush from my backpack for a microphone. "You can be Jane Wiedlin or the drummer."

Jackie makes a face.

She asks, "Why do you always get to be Belinda?"

I answer with my stock reply, "Cause I'm the oldest" and rustle in my backpack and hand Jackie two straws for drums.

At the ticket kiosk a young kid asks Dad, "How many?" Dad holds up two fingers and hands him some crumpled one-dollar bills. We pull into a space close to the screen, pull out our lawn chairs from the back of the shell, and line our chairs up in a row as Dad adjusts the static-filled speakers.

As soon as the movie comes on, no one says a word. We're not allowed to talk during the movies, and we don't want to. Occasionally, we stick our hands into the bag for more popcorn, wiping our oil-stained fingers on the blanket covering our legs. Dad is passed out in the driver's seat by the time the end credits of the second movie roll. Annie shakes him awake and before long he starts up the pickup truck to take us home. Johnny Cash comes on the radio. Dad only swerves a little as he sings along to "I Walk the Line".

When we get home it's after eleven and all the windows are dark. *Mom must be sleeping,* I think to myself. As soon as we walk in the door, Mom is standing there, in her red shirt and black pants. I can't tell if she's mad or not. I whisper to Jackie, "Get ready to run." Annie tiptoes down the hallway to her room. Jackie tenses up beside me.

Mom says in her nice voice, "Girls, did you enjoy the movie?"

I say, "Yeah, Mom, it was great."

Dad says, "Judy, you want me to make you something to eat?"

Mom and Dad sit down at the table. Jackie kisses Dad on the cheek. We never kiss Mom; she doesn't like it. We pad down the hallway, crossing ourselves as we pass the plaster Jesus.

Slipping under my covers, I can hear the oil sizzling as Dad fries up a pork chop for Mom to eat.

The Facts of Life

At home, holidays and parties always result in chaos. They start out good and end bad. The better they are, the worse they end.

Mom wakes us up at seven yelling, "Get up! People are coming over. Get this pigsty cleaned up!"

We're having a pool party and barbecue today. Dad invited over his friends from work.

I pull the covers over my head yelling back, "It's Saturday."

Mom grabs a plastic cup of water from the bathroom and stands over me, holding the cup above my head. I get up, of course.

I walk into the kitchen, Jackie trailing behind me. Annie is already in the kitchen washing dishes.

The house is a wreck as usual. We had promised Mom that we would help her clean the house. The thing Mom loathes the most is laziness. If we ever dare complain, Mom bores us with the all-too-familiar story of her picking strawberries one summer and how it was the hardest summer of her life.

Jackie and Annie start picking up the living room

while I use the vacuum to get all of Whitey's cat hair off the couch. My cat Whitey is a long-haired Persian with snow-white fur and green eyes the color of Oz.

After we finish cleaning the inside of the house, we clean the patio area and the pool. I hoist the handle of the pool net over my shoulder and slide it through the pool while Jackie and Annie sweep the patio area.

The song "Rosanna" by Toto blasts from the speakers of the boom box plugged in at the corner of our backyard. I hear Mom and Dad squabbling already. Their voices echo from their bedroom. Mom's yelling at Dad that he better not get drunk today.

Once the leaves are swept up, the pool looks like clean blue sky. The tile on the pool is dark blue with gold specks. Mom and Dad had put the pool in after we begged them. They had to take something called a second on the house. I have no idea what a second is. I love my pool. I am at peace underwater.

Richard and his wife arrive to the pool party at noon along with their two kids. Richard works with Dad at Mayflower. Dad used to drive eighteen-wheeler trucks long distance, but he gave it up so that he could spend more time at home. Richard is darkly handsome, with a thick head of hair.

"He looks like Ponch from 'CHIPS,'" I whisper to Jackie.

"CHIPS" is our favorite show on TV. It comes on at three p.m., and we run home from school every day to turn on the TV so we don't miss the opening theme song.

A little later, my dad's friend Johnny R and his wife

arrive with their kids.

"John, how you doing?" Johnny R says, slapping Dad's hand. Dad hands him a beer.

Mom grimaces when he walks into the backyard and mutters, "The drunk is here."

I strut around in my new yellow bikini with ties on the side. Jackie is wearing a blue-and-pink bikini and Annie has on a one-piece. My sisters and I always have an unofficial competition for which one of us can get the darkest. We're half Mexican so we can get super dark. After we sunbathe for an hour slathered in baby oil, we pull down our bathing suit straps to see who has the most dramatic tan.

Later that afternoon, I relax on a blue plastic blow-up floater reading. I slather more baby oil all over myself until I glisten like a baby seal. The sun warms my brown skin. It feels like the most beautiful day in the world.

As I paddle the floater along the side of the pool, Jackie tries to knock me over. I slap her away and shout, "Stop it. You're being a shithead."

Jackie looks at me. I think I hurt her feelings until she sticks her tongue out and makes a funny face.

"Pull me," I say in my bossy, oldest-twin voice. Jackie obeys and swims as fast as she can, tugging me along in my floater. We move along the edge of the pool, making up stories about a fake world like the one with puppets in Mister Roger's Neighborhood. We've been watching the show since we were really little. Jackie and I love puppets.

"That's the enchanted land," I explain to Jackie, as we pass by the planter with the geraniums in it. "Fairies live in there." Jackie smiles. She loves make-believe.

Jackie has the best imagination of all of us and always pretends her stuffed Disneyland Pot Belly Bear can talk.

After a while, I flip myself over. The water is cool, not cold. I swim the length of the pool underwater, holding my breath the entire time like a mermaid. I wish I could hold my breath and stay underwater forever.

Later, all the kids jump off the diving board one at a time and swim past each other, while the other kids laugh and wrestle. I organize a game of Marco Polo.

"Marco," I shout with my eyes closed. Whenever I hear a voice say "Polo," I follow the voice and tag someone. I get out of the pool after the game and towel myself dry.

Dad is in front of the grill in his usual blue swim trunks and a T-shirt, his white skin burnt bright red from the sun. Dad always hates wearing shorts because his legs are so swollen from his job moving furniture. Dad is on at least his seventh or eighth Budweiser. It's hard to keep track, he drinks them so fast.

Annie sneaks up behind him and, in one gulp, she downs the rest of the can he had left sitting on the picnic table.

Dad swipes at her and says in a laughing voice, "Annie, don't do that."

Johnny R grins when Dad says, "She loves beer just like her daddy."

I watch as Dad crumples his can, and I run and hand him and Johnny cold beers out of the cooler. Richard walks over and they all toast.

"Thanks, Jenny, that's my girl," Dad says with a relaxed smile, his blue eyes twinkling.

Mom walks outside, her arms folded across her chest. I can tell she is pissed that Dad is drinking so much. Her curly short black hair is pulled back with a brown headband. Her dark skin stands out against her white tank top and white shorts.

"Slow down, John, don't get all borracho," Mom says to him with a glare.

Dad opens another beer and teases her, trying to get her to laugh.

"C'mon, Judy, relax," he says in a slurred voice. I can tell his teasing is beginning to get on her nerves.

Johnny R's wife turns to Mom with a smile and says, "How's work, Judy?"

Everyone knows Mom is a waitress at a Chinese restaurant in town. Mom's smile is a bit forced as she shrugs and says, "Same old, same old. Edna won't buy us anything for the restaurant and Robin wants every weekend off. That's why I have the late shift tonight."

Johnny R walks around to face Mom, wraps his arm around her shoulders, and says, "C'mon, Judy, have a good time. Calm down and have a beer."

Uh oh, I think to myself. *Mom won't like that comment.*

Mom looks at him. She wiggles out of his grasp with an exasperated look and says, "OK, Johnny, should I drink a twelve-pack and drive to work?"

Dad and Johnny R crack up, drunk on more than laughter. Mom turns away with a grunt. "Pendejo drunks," she mutters, and walks inside, slamming the door.

I watch as Dad places huge steaks on the grill four at a time. Smoke rises from the glowing embers. As an adult, I will remember those steaks and my mouth will water.

"C'mon, girls, time to eat," he yells when the steaks are done. Jackie and I fight each other for the front of the line and as we walk up, Dad places a steak on each of our paper plates.

"Put some of that Worcestershire sauce on there," Dad says, handing me the bottle. I sprinkle it on top of the steak.

"And get some of my famous mustard potato salad," he adds. "I made one without onions for Annie."

Dad cracks open another beer and sways as he serves out the steaks.

Mom stands by the screen door, glaring at him as he downs his beer. I can tell that she is getting more and more angry. My stomach tightens.

"Mom, come and eat," I say with a smile, trying to ease the tension. Mom walks over slowly to make herself a plate. She swipes Dad's hand away as he pulls at her.

"Stop it, John, I want to eat. I gotta go to work later," she says in a short voice.

Dad bulges his eyes out, which always makes her laugh. He pulls her down next to him at the picnic table.

The fatty sides of my rib-eye steak poke off the edges of my plate.

My sisters and I crowd together at the far end of the picnic table and shovel spoonful after spoonful of potato salad into our mouths. We guzzle can after can of grape Shasta cola. After we finish eating and guzzling soda, I burp as loud as I can. Jackie follows my burp with a louder burp of her own. Annie grimaces and hands us napkins to wipe our faces and hands. Even though Annie is the youngest, she makes us mind our manners.

I turn and see that Mom and Dad are not at the table anymore. *Uh oh*, I think to myself.

I see them in the living room, fighting, their images a bit distorted through the glass patio door. I ease toward the door to listen.

Mom yells at Dad, "You're drunk, John. You're a goddamn filthy drunk. You promised you would keep it together today. Now you're fucking drunk as usual."

Dad yells back, "Why do you always gotta ruin everything, Judy?"

I can almost feel it coming. I watch Mom slap at Dad. My stomach is hurting and I can feel the steak sitting in the pit of my stomach like a dead weight.

A few minutes later, Mom emerges from the house with her crazy "Don't mess with me" look in her eyes.

"It's time for you to go," Mom says to everyone.

No one pays her any attention; everyone is talking and eating.

Mom starts shrieking louder and louder, "Time to go!"

When no one pays her attention, she screams in a loud banshee voice, "Get the fuck out!"

Everyone turns to look at Mom. It turns quiet.

"Cuckoo, cuckoo," Jackie says in my ear. I nudge her quiet.

Johnny R's wife shakes her head as they pack up their stuff and walk out the back gate without a word. Richard and his wife glance at us with a worried look as they leave next, with kids in tow. I think, *This is so embarrassing*.

Mom stands there, hands on her hips, waiting for everyone to go.

"Shit, here it goes again," Jackie says softly. I nod my head.

Annie is shaking in her swimsuit like a scared little rabbit. I grab her towel and put it around her shoulders.

Mom and Dad go inside. I hear them screaming at one another and throwing things, the soundtrack to my childhood.

A tear rolls down Annie's face. I wrap my arm around her. Jackie grabs her hand. Us three girls sit in a circle around the jacuzzi just waiting for it to be over.

The window to Mom and Dad's bedroom looks out onto the pool, and we all place our faces against the glass and watch Mom beat on Dad with her fists. Dad turns around and pushes Mom into the wall head first. Mom clutches her face. She's crying. Mom's hurt. My stomach lurches and I feel like I'm gonna throw up.

Jackie, Annie, and I gather around the picnic table.

"Should we go?" Jackie asks.

"Just wait, it might be over soon," I say trying to stay calm.

Jackie and Annie sit down by the pool with their feet in the water.

But this time, they don't stop fighting. Dad runs out of the back door with Mom right after him. Mom throws a plate at him and then a mug. Shards of glass litter the patio floor.

"Get the fuck out of here, John," Mom screams as she clutches her face. Mom's eye looks swollen.

I hear Dad's pickup truck revving up and then more screaming as he pulls away. I think to myself, *He shouldn't be driving.*

Minutes later, Mom races back into the backyard from the side gate and screams, "Get out of here, girls." Mom always kicks us out after they fight. Tears are running down her face.

She never needs to tell us twice. If we stay, it could get ugly.

Annie runs out the back gate first and streaks down the street in her towel and swimsuit. Jackie races to catch her and I follow. I make sure to grab my book.

John Galvin Park is right around the corner. A slightly rusted swing set sits on dried-out grass, along with a monkey-bar set and a large, circular maze that looks like a big piece of orange cheese. I go to my usual place inside the plastic cheese. I like the twisting holed walls even though it smells like pee sometimes. My head is swimming as if I am still underwater.

Jackie pushes Annie on the swing. Her hair trails behind like a fan.

The higher Jackie pushes her, the more Annie giggles.

I look back down at my book and think, I wonder if everyone's life is like this.

Jackie waves her hand at me, a sign she wants me to come over to her. I wipe my face and close my book. Walking out to the swings, I wince as I see Mom's brown Pinto drive by. I point at her car. Jackie and Annie nod at me in unison.

Mom pulls over and motions for us to come over.

We walk over and when we get closer, she yells, "I called in sick and I'm going to go find your dad. Go home." She seems calmer. Under her eye, the red is turning to blue.

We stay at the park. I watch the sun set from inside my

plastic cheese and wonder why good days always have to go bad. I wish I was someone else, anyone but me.

Hours later, I hear Mom's voice echoing over the street to the park, "Girls, come back. Please come back."

The three of us take our time walking, in a single-file line, back home.

Private School Girls

When we were in fifth grade, Mom decided we needed to be in Catholic school. There was a Catholic school at Saint George's, the church off Euclid by Mom's work. My sisters and I were pissed off by her decision because we would have to make new friends. We had attended the same elementary school since first grade. I thought to myself, *This is going to upset everything.* Plus, who wanted to go to school with a bunch of rich kids whose parents could afford private school? Mom always said we were bill-poor. Why did she want to spend her money on this?

"Mom, why can't we just stay where we are?" I pleaded with her. Jackie and Annie nodded along. "Yeah, Mom, why?" Annie chimed in. Jackie made it a trio. "Yeah, Mom, why?"

We liked attending public school and we liked our after-school routine. Every day after school, we would go over to my best friend Melinda's house. Her mom Mary watched us most afternoons.

Mary was born in Mexico and, unlike my mom, she knew how to cook. Her homemade pozole was a spicy combination of pork and hominy with shredded cabbage and a touch of lime. Mary would feed us the soup in small ceramic bowls with homemade tortillas on the side. The flavorful soup was a sharp change from the prepackaged macaroni and cheese Mom made or the beef roasts and gray vegetables that Dad cooked.

"Sientate," Mary would say, and all us girls would crowd around her tiny kitchen table slurping our bowls of soup. "Sabroso?" she always asked. We would all nod as we dunked our tortillas and gulped the soup.

After our snack, we walked to the liquor store on the corner to buy the salted plums covered with chili powder that Melinda had introduced to us.

Melinda and I had been best friends since elementary school. She was born in Mexico and spoke Spanish. Even back then she was a clotheshorse. One of the first times I spoke to Melinda, she said to me, "Everyone says you're smart," with a smile. She raised an eyebrow as she stared at the green frog T-shirt that I had paired with blue flared Dittos and said, "But what are you wearing?"

Melinda shopped at Mervyn's and looked down at our Kmart clothes. Everyone wanted to be friends with Melinda, and I desperately wanted her to like me. She was everything I was not. She had straight black hair that she wore spiked up, and perfect bronze-colored skin. She favored jean jackets and tight jeans and was the epitome of cool. Melinda was also bossy, sarcastic, and popular with the boys.

The first time she invited me and Jackie over her house after school, I tried to act nonchalant by saying, "Sure, Mel…" when I felt like screaming yes. Mom forced us to let

Annie tag along because it turned out that Melinda had a little sister named Pamela that was Annie's age.

Melinda and Pamela lived with their parents in an apartment down the street from us in Ontario. Melinda's mom Mary was in her early twenties and lonely because she didn't drive, and Melinda's dad Arturo was always at work. After a couple of visits, Mary started watching my sisters and me almost every day because Mom didn't want us home alone after school while she worked.

Mary and Mom became friends. If Mom got off early, she would come by and sit with Mary in the kitchen drinking cup after cup of coffee and talking in Spanish. Melinda would make me laugh by mimicking how Mom put spoonful after spoonful of sugar in her coffee. If Mom didn't get off early, Dad would pick us up when he got off his shift at the moving company. Dad was often late and would drive up in his pickup truck with the smell of beer on his breath. Mary would shake her head and say, "John, you're borracho. Can you drive?" Dad would wave her off and load us into the car, swerving to country music the whole way home.

I didn't bring friends home very often because if Mom was having a bad day, she would tell people off. Melinda and Pamela became the exception to that rule because they handled Mom's varying moods with ease and didn't react when Mom yelled.

Melinda and I didn't talk about race at all. We knew we were brown. It was obvious. I especially loved hearing Melinda talk Spanish to her mom even though she was hesitant to do so. Melinda wanted her mom to learn English. But I was jealous of this secret other world of rolled-out Rs.

We rode our bikes for hours around the neighborhood. Our favorite thing to do was to go to Pup 'n' Taco and pool our change on twenty-five-cent taco day. We never had enough money for a drink, so we sipped water from their tiny paper cups as we closed our eyes and bit into their crispy shells, the sauce and cheese dripping down our chins. In the late afternoon, we would hang out at the baseball park and watch the boys play as we smoked the cigarettes we had bought with a forged note from the same liquor store by Melinda's house. Sometimes, we would steal one of Mary's wine coolers and drink it under the bleachers, hiding from our little sisters, who trailed us around and who were always looking for ways to tattle on us.

The debate continued about Catholic school all summer. Finally, Mom put her foot down, looked at us, and shook her head. "You girls need to focus on school and church and stop running around like locas. Going to church will be good for you. A lot of the kids at this school end up going to college. I want you girls to go to school and be someone, not just a waitress like me. Education is everything. So stop complaining, dammit. It's gonna cost me all my tips every month. I don't even know how we're going to afford all the goddamn uniforms."

Mom always told us how she prayed to God to give her kids after she lost her son David. When she got pregnant with us twins, she said it was God answering her prayers. She promised God that she would take her girls to church every Sunday.

Mom worked a lot on the weekends and worked late on Saturday nights, but she always took us to church at least every other Sunday, made us dress pretty, and gave us each a quarter to put in the collection tray. When we were younger, she made us do our catechism classes and bought us beautiful white dresses for our First Communions. Everyone at church loved Mom. She had a lot of friends and they would always say, "Hi, Judy" and bring us girls treats.

"Mom, that school's gonna cost a lot of money," I said with a rueful grin. I was trying to prey on her frugality. But Mom was not buying it and retorted, "Didn't I just say that?"

Despite our protests, Mom enrolled us in private school but promised we could visit Melinda and Pamela on the weekends. When the school found out that Mom waitressed, they gave her a low-income discount, charging her one hundred dollars a month tuition for all three of us. Even with the discount, the tuition was still a stretch. Uniforms were required, a gray-and-red checkered skirt and a white, short-sleeved, button-down shirt. Mom bought us used uniforms to save money. I wanted a red sweater with the logo to go over the shirt, but Mom said they were too expensive and that she could find cheaper ones at Zodys or Kmart.

"My skirt's faded and too long, and the shirt's uncomfortable," Jackie said. The white shirt bulged a bit against her chest, a tiny bit too tight. My skirt was too big at the waist and too long, so Mom took it in with uneven stitches. Annie's skirt magically seemed to fit just right.

We kept up our complaining until Mom told us that we were ungrateful brats who needed to stop our bitching. But she patted us on the head when she said it.

The first months were hard in the new school. The

nuns were stern and church was mandatory every day. Even worse, I had to play volleyball, which I was inept at. No matter how hard I tried, I couldn't hold my arms right to bounce the ball off my wrist, and I always ducked whenever the ball came at me.

A pretty blonde girl named Laura, who was the captain of the volleyball team, invited Jackie and me to a slumber party at her house. Laura's dad was a doctor and everyone knew she was rich. She lived in a huge Spanish-style house. Laura looked just like Blair Warner from "The Facts of Life."

There was a girl in our class who always made fun of me. I don't remember her name. All I remember was that she was chubby with blonde hair. We got into a fight at the slumber party and she called me a spic wetback. I knew *spic* was a racial slur, but I didn't know what it meant. I knew what *wetback* meant. I had heard Dad's friends use the insult. Mom hated those friends of his and said they were a bunch of white-trash drunks who were a bad influence on Dad. I looked at the girl and yelled back, "You're a fat bitch and I'm half white." I don't know why I said that. But I had to say something.

The *spic* and *wetback* slurs stuck in my mind during my time at Saint George's. I would sometimes look down at my faded uniform and wish it was bright and new and the right length.

When Mom told us that the school was too much money and that we would be back in public school for our seventh-grade year, we cheered. I was so relieved. I wanted to spend my days hanging out with Melinda, riding bikes with her after school, eating her mom's pozole, and then walking to the liquor store to buy cigarettes. Melinda knew my dad was a white drunk man, and that my Mexican mom was crazy. She didn't care, and neither did I.

Dolly's House

I wish I could go to my friend Dolly's house, but I'm on restriction for getting caught with a pack of cigarettes. Mom and Dad aren't good about enforcing punishments like restriction. I'm sure I'll be off restriction by the weekend.

Dolly lives in the brand-new condos next to Imperial Junior High, where we go to school. Her mom always leaves us the best snacks, and we sneak off campus at lunch and go stuff ourselves on chips and dip and cheese and crackers. Their condo is so cool-looking, and super fancy with Southwest furniture in coral, pink, and blue. Dolly's family moved here from the South and uses words like "fixin'." We have a lot in common. Dolly and I both love Duran Duran and the movie *Sixteen Candles* and want to dress like Molly Ringwald.

I just transferred in from Saint George's, a parochial school in Ontario that we attended for two years. Mom couldn't afford the tuition or the uniforms so we started seventh grade back at public school. I was happy because my best friend Melinda and me would be reunited again. The band Wham! U.K. was all the rage, and I remember my outfit on the first day of school: black leggings and a florescent pink oversized sweatshirt like the one in Wham's video. Mom bought Jackie the same sweater only in yellow, and I begged Jackie not to wear it the first day.

The first day of school I realized that Melinda and I didn't have any classes together. All of my classes were gifted honors classes. Melinda and I talked about it and we promised each other we would still eat lunch together at least twice a week.

My first class was English, and I sat in the front of the class as usual. A girl sat down next to me and said, "Hi, my name is Dolly. What's yours?" in a thick Southern twang. Dolly and I became fast friends.

Dolly has curly blonde hair and wears her bangs over her face on a slant. "It's New Ro!" she tells me. I pretend I know what she means, but later she explains that "New Ro" is short for the New Romantic music phase, which includes bands like Duran Duran and Adam and the Ants. She wears the coolest white overalls that have splashes of florescent faux paint splattered all over them.

I often go to Dolly's house at lunch and watch movies with her on the cable channel. Her room is covered in pictures of Duran Duran. She always says she is going to marry the bass player, John Taylor. The lead singer, Simon Le Bon, is always my choice.

Dolly and I are close. I sometimes spend the night at her house and her mom gets us takeout. Her mom's bathroom cabinet is filled with medication for her "issues."

"She takes Valium to calm her nerves," Dolly told me one day, her voice twanging on the word "nerves."

My friendship with Dolly will eventually fade. By high school, she will move back to the South and won't go on to Chaffey with us. I wonder, where she is now?

If I was writing a novel, it would go something like this: Dolly moved back to the South and graduated from high school early and went on to study film at NYU. She changed her name when she became a famous filmmaker. But this is real life, and I have no idea where she is now.

Weaving Roads

It's eight o'clock and Dad's still not home from work. Mom is making one phone call after another to the bars around town. I am working on my *Romeo and Juliet* book report on the sofa. The report, for my seventh-grade honors English class, is due tomorrow. I have spent hours on the report. I've read *Romeo and Juliet* three times. Shakespeare knew his shit. *Romeo and Juliet* is my favorite Shakespeare play. Unlike most people, I like the fact that there is not a happy ending. It's more like real life.

Mom yells into the receiver, "Is John Mantz there? This is his wife, Judy. Have you seen him? Well, if he comes in, tell him to call me."

After about five of those calls, Mom throws the telephone against the wall and starts pacing the house. I jump up from the sofa. My heart is pounding.

"There goes another phone," Jackie says louder than she should. Jackie always argues with Mom.

I put my fingers against my lips and shake my head at Jackie. She knows that this is my "not a good idea" head shake.

"He's probably with that drunk Johnny at a bar with a bunch of other lowlifes," Mom says as she picks up the busted phone from the floor.

I nod. She's probably right, but I am too afraid to say so in case it sets her off.

Jackie is watching "Good Times."

"Turn it off," Mom says with a glare that means she is serious. "I hate that show. It's all about the ghetto. Why do you want to watch that?"

We know better than to protest even though it was our favorite episode of "Good Times," the one where Penny, played by Janet Jackson, gets taken away from her abusive mother and moves in with the neighbor Willona.

Mom starts ranting again, "Leaving me alone with you kids while he's out getting drunk. My brother Roland told me not to marry him. Said he was a borracho."

What the hell does she want me to say? Mom's brothers dislike Dad. Mom says it's because he's a drunk. I think it's because he's a white cowboy who doesn't speak Spanish. It reminds me of the way Romeo's and Juliet's families refuse to let them be together, but in this case, Mom's family is right. Mom and Dad are bad for one another. Some might say cursed.

Mom looks at me. I shrug. When she looks away, Jackie pinches me and points out the door like we should run. I know why we can't and mouth "Annie" at her. Jackie sighs out loud and hunches over and puts her head in her hands. Annie is Mom's favorite.

"Annie, Annie, Annie!" Mom screams out the screen door into the backyard. Annie doesn't answer.

"Mom, she's probably in her room," I say hopping off the couch. I run down the hall into Annie's room.

Annie is hiding in her usual spot on the side of her bed against the wall playing with her Baby Fresh Doll. I love Annie's long straight hair and run my hand down her silky, perfectly combed tresses. Her hair is straight and beautiful like Juliet's. Mom says she got Dad's white-people hair. Jackie and I have short, kinky, curly hair. Annie looks up at me and smiles. She's only ten to our twelve, but she is neat and organized.

"Annie," I whisper, grabbing her by the arm to pull her up. "You're gonna make it worse. Come on." Annie pulls away.

"Annie, you get out here," Mom screams.

I push Annie down the hallway toward the kitchen. Mom is pulling at her hair. That's never a good sign. Mom grabs her keys and says, "I'm done, I'm leaving him. C'mon, let's go, Annie."

She's going to leave without us again. I look at Annie's face and she looks like a scared little rabbit. I can feel one of my headaches coming on.

What if Mom drives crazy and they die in a car accident? Anything can happen when Mom is in one of her moods. I decide to speak up.

"Mom…."

Mom interrupts me, "You twins are coming, too. We can go stay with my brother. Go pack some things."

I look down at my book report. It's not finished; I still need to add a couple paragraphs and the conclusion. But there's nothing I can do. To bring it up would just make Mom angry and I don't want her to leave without me and Jackie. I look at Jackie and mouth "Hurry up." Jackie and I rush to our bedroom.

"Annie was a good baby. She never cried. Not like you twins." Mom often says. Mom says Annie reminds her of her mother, who died when Mom was fourteen. Mom always says that Annie has a sweet disposition. I sometimes picture Mom getting in a car accident and her Pinto catching on fire with Annie inside. The thought of it makes my stomach hurt.

"She's going nuts," Jackie says. "She's getting worse. It's no wonder Dad doesn't want to come home." I nod, knowing she's right, and say, "C'mon, just hurry and pack."

"And don't fight with her," I warn Jackie. Jackie shrugs her shoulders. Jackie knows she sets Mom off. Jackie makes Mom see red, probably because she's Dad's favorite.

I stuff a pair of underwear and jeans in my backpack and grab a couple of dog-eared novels. I run out of the room as I hear Mom revving the engine of her Pinto. Jackie follows close behind. As we run out of the house, we see that Mom is already backing out of the driveway. The day is gray and overcast and casts our cul-de-sac in shadow. A couple of the neighbor boys are outside and looking our way. I hope they didn't hear Mom cussing.

Annie is scooting down in the front seat, hiding from the neighbor boys' prying eyes. Mom yells, "Annie, sit up straight!" Annie sits up.

I wave at Mom to stop the car. I yank open the door and slide into the back seat with Jackie right beside me. Mom screeches off. Our neighborhood flies by. Mom speeds past John Galvin Park, the one we always run to when she kicks us out. My friend Christy lives in the Section Eight apartments across the street. Mom runs a red light at Grove and takes the on-ramp to the I-10 toward Los Angeles. She keeps muttering under her breath, "Leaving me with the kids all the time."

I want to scream at her to shut up, but I don't because she's liable to hit one of us and lose control of the car if I do. Instead, I stay quiet and open my book. I hate reading in the car, it makes me carsick, but it takes my mind off things.

After reading for a couple of minutes, I get a headache. When I tell my mom I am feeling carsick, she just makes a face and doesn't pull over to get me a 7UP like she would if she was in a good mood. She tells me to roll down the window and breathe in the wind. Hoping I don't puke, I roll down the window and gulp in the hot air.

We reach the 57 freeway, which leads to Orange County. We pass Brea and then Fullerton. Jackie and I make faces at people in cars and have to pinch each other to keep from laughing out loud at their reactions.

As we pass Anaheim Stadium, the car jerks suddenly to a stop and Mom yells and pounds the steering wheel. She turns the radio station to the traffic report. The announcer says that the 57 freeway is backed up due to an accident. The traffic eases up a bit and Mom gets off on Katella Avenue, the Disneyland exit, and me and my sisters marvel at the Matterhorn in the distance. Its fake snow-covered peaks are visible from the street.

"Space Mountain is better than the Matterhorn," Jackie says in a matter-of-fact voice.

"No way, the Matterhorn is better," I retort. "Plus,

there's a snow monster. Space Mountain doesn't have a snow monster."

"Yeah, but Space Mountain is way faster," Jackie replies. "Way faster. Right, Annie?"

Annie turns to look at both of us and says in a quacking Donald Duck voice, "I like Space Mountain."

Jackie and I start laughing hysterically. We love her Donald Duck voice—neither of us can do it. Annie will never do it on command, no matter if we beg her, not even if we hit her. She only does it when she wants to. Annie starts doing the voice again saying, "I love Disneyland" over and over, moving her head from side to side. We clutch ourselves in giggles.

Mom screeches, "Girls, be quiet!"

I put down my book and lay my head against the window. I doze and dream about being on a terrace, waiting for Romeo to climb up and save me. The minute I wake up, I realize I left my book report at home.

Now it is dark outside. We are on the downhill slope of an unfamiliar mountain road. The road twists and turns and Mom cusses up a storm as she rides the brakes.

Mom shouts as she turns the wheel. I can smell the brakes and make the mistake of asking Jackie what the smell is. Hearing my question, Mom twists her head like the girl in *The Exorcist* to look at us. Spit flies out of her mouth as she says "It's your dad's fault we're lost."

I know I shouldn't say anything, but can't seem to stop myself from asking her, "Where are we?" Mom gives me another glare in the mirror.

"It looks like Sleepy Hollow," Jackie says.

Jackie's right, it does look like something out of a book. There are large trees lining the roads and old houses that look like houses in a fairy tale. The car swerves into the wrong lane and another car comes around the turn, almost sideswiping us. Annie screams and Mom pulls over to the side of the road. She brakes quickly, stops the car, and gets out.

I watch as Mom walks down the dark road away from us. I can hear her crying through the glass.

"Where is she going?" Jackie says, "She's a nutcase. She's gonna get hit by a car."

"Or a car will hit us," I say, as I reach over the front seat to turn on the hazard lights.

Annie is whispering a Hail Mary. I cross myself and bow my head. In what seems like an hour, but is probably much less, Mom comes back. When I look at her, Mom smiles and starts the car. Jackie is about to say something to Mom, but I poke her into silence. In less than ten minutes, we are sitting at a roadside coffee house, drinking hot chocolate. Mom says that she called her brother from the pay phone and knows where she is going now.

When we get to her brother Roland's house in Buena Park, it's late. His wife Sara opens the door and says in a welcoming voice, "Mijas. We have the sleeping bags out for you." I smile at her.

My aunt Sara is always welcoming. My teenage cousin Carol, who is her youngest daughter, runs up and gives all of us a big hug. My headache eases. Mom and Sara sit at her dining-room table speaking Spanish. I can tell that they are talking about Dad. Aunt Sara is telling Mom that we can live with them. Mom is shaking her head no. "I love him," Mom says in Spanish. After a little while, Mom is in a better mood and laughs and jokes about Dad's carousing.

Carol helps Annie with her sleeping bag while Jackie places hers by the fireplace. I lay my sleeping bag underneath the pool table and stare up at the bottom of the pool table thinking about my book report.

***

The next morning, I am in my English class. My teacher is going from desk to desk collecting reports. My book report is at home. I thought we would have time to go home and get my report, but we didn't have time. Mom just dropped us off and wouldn't listen when I told her I needed something. She was late for her shift at the restaurant.

My teacher is couple of desks away from me. What do I say? Should I say the truth?

"Jenny," my teacher says with an expectant nod holding out her hand. I am never late with my homework. Maybe it would have been better if we had crashed. Then I would have a good excuse for not having my book report. I choose to stay silent and shake my head and look down at my feet. Maybe she will pass me by and talk to me about it later.

"Jenny," she says again tapping me on my shoulder. She is a nice lady but super strict about deadlines. "Is your report in your bag?" I shake my head again and my eyes well up with tears. This sucks. All the GATE kids are looking at me.

"I had a bad night. I forgot it at home," I stammer. "I had to go to Orange County and....."

"You don't have it?" she asks. She seems surprised.

Didn't I just tell her that? I didn't sleep last night. My head is pounding and I keep picturing the book report sitting on my desk. This is not my fault. I look at her and raise my eyebrows and say "No" with the O drawn out.

All the kids in class laugh and my teacher shakes her head at me. "I'll see you after class," she says. She does not look happy. After class, she sits down across from me and says in a kind voice, "Jenny, you can turn the paper in tomorrow. I won't penalize your grade because you have never been late. Is something going on at home?"

My head clears, and I want to tell her all about it but don't know how.

"Just the usual," I say with a shrug as I grab my bag and get up from the chair. "I promise I will turn it in first thing tomorrow. It's already done. I really appreciate it."

If I hug her, I'll cry. Instead, I turn and rush out the door with a wave.

The Big O

My parents bought a bar called The Big O. Dad calls it a tavern. The sign has a big fat O on it. The Big O is a mile away from our house in Ontario on Holt and Grove.

Mom didn't want Dad to buy the bar, but Dad convinced her.

"Why that bar, John? Isn't Holt Street where all the hookers hang out?" Mom said when Dad first brought up the idea.

Dad ignored the hooker comment. He was on a mission.

"It's a dream, Judy," Dad said. "There's pool tables, a pinball machine, video games, and it already has a beer and wine license. They are even going to pay us to manage the trailer park behind it."

Mom huffed and puffed, "No way, John. No way!"

"This could be a moneymaker, Judy," Dad said, trying to cajole her.

Mom was a yeller and a fighter. She didn't handle fools lightly. Mom knew that anytime you put the words "trailer park" and "bar" together, it was trouble. She also knew that

Dad loved his Budweiser, which was the sorest point of contention in their debate over Dad's quest to buy The Big O.

Mom looked daggers at him, her voice getting higher and higher, "No, no, no! I mean it! Dammit, John, you are going to end up drunk all day and land us in the poorhouse. I don't want to lose the house, and if you quit your job and buy that money pit, that's what will happen,"

Dad shrugged his head and said, "C'mon, Judy, please. Let's do it. I promise not to drink too much. There's a jukebox. We can put a lot of country on the jukebox and make it a honky-tonk. Patsy Cline, Johnny Cash, Waylon Jennings...."

Jackie popped her head up from the couch like a jack-in-the-box, interrupting their conversation.

"Dad, can you put the Go-Go's on the jukebox?"

Mom glared her into silence and Jackie slipped back into the couch. I giggled softly, gave her a high five, and whispered into her ear: "Let's ask for Pat Benatar, too."

"C'mon, Judy," Dad said as he kissed her cheek. He put his arm around her shoulders as if they were about to dance. "I've dreamed about this for years. It's a once-in-a-lifetime opportunity."

Dad had always dreamed of owning either a bar or a donut shop. He had been talking about it since I could walk. Dad's two favorite things were beer and junk food... oh, and country music.

I don't know...," Mom said, her voice trailing off. "It has always been your dream. But you have no idea how to manage a business, John."

I could hear a note of give in Mom's voice. She was

leaving the door open just a little. Why was she even considering this? I was a kid and could see it was a bad idea. Dad loved to drink and hang out with what Mom calls "the lowlifes."

But we all knew down deep inside that Dad was going to make the bar happen no matter the cost.

***

Buying the bar was just like the time Dad bought a freezer full of steaks from some kid walking around the block. When Mom found out that not only had he bought the meat but a freezer to house it in, she hit the roof.

"John, you're an idiot," Mom told him.

She continued on, screaming at him. "John, you got taken. You're one of those suckers born every minute. The bill is for almost a thousand dollars. Where are we going to get that kind of money? We could have a bought a car. That's a couple months of house payments."

Dad always made a face like his stomach hurt when Mom started yelling at him. "I'll make the payments," Dad assured her with a grimace and a shake of his head.

"We will get the best steaks, Judy. There's a ton of porterhouses and filet minions." (Dad was not known for his proper pronunciations.)

"Dammit, John, what are we going to do with all those steaks? There are enough steaks for an army." Mom asked.

"Judy, we'll eat them. With the discount for buying the freezer, the steaks are the same price as chicken or hamburger. The girls will eat them, too. They love good steaks just like their Daddy," Dad had said.

Jackie and I had nodded in unison. We did love good

steaks. On summer days, Dad would fire up his charcoal grill and make us each a big fat steak. We didn't like to share.

Mom shook her head. "Why'd you have to buy the freezer? We're not rich, John. You're a truck driver, and I'm a goddamn waitress."

"The freezer was part of the deal. The freezer is restaurant quality. We'll eat like kings," Dad had said. "The kid who came to the door said everyone on the block bought one. We can have a block barbecue."

"Block barbecue?" Mom had said, shaking her head. "No one else bought one. You're a fool. My brother said you were a dumb gringo, but I didn't believe him."

"Judy, I don't want to fight. I'll send the freezer back," Dad said with his stock sigh and shrug. Dad knew he couldn't win by arguing with Mom. The better strategy was to make her feel bad.

Dad looked at her with sad eyes, "It's your decision, Judy. I'm sorry. I just wanted good meat for the family."

"Are you gonna pay it?" Mom had said.

Dad pleaded, knowing he was almost there. "I'll pay it. I promise, Judy. And I'll make some of my potato salad to go with those filet minions. You'll eat it."

"Fine, John," Mom said giving in like she always did. "John, you're making the payment."

It worked. Another hair-brained idea had been approved. Within three months, Mom was making the fifty-dollar payment. Eventually, some men came and knocked on the door and showed Mom and Dad a piece of paper and the freezer was taken away. Mom said it was repossessed. They couldn't take the steaks because they were already in our stomachs.

***

Just like with the freezer full of meat, Dad made the bar happen, and within mere months of first talking about it, Mom and Dad were the owners of a bar on Holt Street bordering a trailer park in the worst part of Ontario.

The bar always smelled like stale cigarettes and old tap beer. My parents couldn't afford a full alcohol license so all they served was wine and beer. Dad would get plastered every night he tended bar. Patrons would buy him drinks all night. He would stumble into the house at two a.m. and Mom would scream at him, "I told you this was going to happen, John!"

Dad would take us to the bar with him every Saturday morning. We would clean the dark green felt of the pool tables with a brush, and steal cigarettes from the machine. "What do you girls wanna eat?" Dad always asked. "We have frozen pizza or hamburgers and fries." Dad didn't care that it was only nine in the morning. I would always choose cheese pizza, and Dad let me put songs on the jukebox. He had Alabama, Waylon Jennings, Willie Nelson and, of course, Johnny Cash and Loretta Lynn along with a ton of other country music. Even though Mom was Mexican, she loved country music. Her favorite was Freddy Fender. I loved watching Mom dress up in her Western jean suit to go out with Dad to the bar. "We met at a honky-tonk," Mom would remind us. "I always had a thing for white-man cowboys."

My sisters and I never listened to country. Country was for truckers like my dad. And hillbillies. We preferred

Pat Benatar, the Go-Go's, and Olivia Newton-John.

Dad taught us how to play pool at the bar. Dad would stomp out his Kent cigarette, chalk his hands, and lean over the table, holding his pool stick in a confident way, making sure to take careful aim before taking his shot. We would play pinball for hours. We never wanted to leave. We played our turns in silence, with focus. Dad loved to hit the machine with his hip. "You're gonna tilt it, Dad," we would scream. Dad only tilted one time out of ten, but he came close most of the time.

Jackie and I would fight over who got to clean the pool table, but no one wanted to mop the floor. Annie would whine, "I'm not tall enough, Daddy."

Dad would grumble, "Give your ol' man a break, girls." Dad's knees were bad from years of moving furniture, and his legs would swell. Dad even had to wear special blood-pressure socks. It hurt him a lot, and he would wince in pain, but he mopped anyway, while humming along to the sounds of the Oak Ridge Boys.

The Challenge

I walk into my honors English class. The room is already full—all the front rows are taken. I sigh in frustration realizing I will be stuck in the back and I forgot my glasses. But thankfully, being near-sighted, I can still read without my glasses, and I have Judy Blume's *Wifey* in my backpack. I've been dying to read it. The book is being passed around in secret because of the steamy sex scenes.

There's a middle seat in the back row next to my friend Rose. I dump my ratty, stained backpack next to the seat and crack my neck. My head hurts. Last night, I only slept a couple of hours. Mom and Dad fought all night. I can almost hear the sound of their dishes crashing against the wall as I stare out the window of my class. The sky is a pretty bright blue, and the clouds look fake, like white, puffy marshmallows. Today will be a good day.

The bell rings, signaling the start of class. The door opens, and a maintenance man in a gray shirt wheels in a television with an orange extension cord dragging behind it. The TV is a large, wood-paneled Zenith, just like the one we have at home. The maintenance man plugs it in. After a minute, the screen comes on.

Miss G walks up, turns the channel on the TV, and gives a little jump. She claps her hands and says, like a little kid on Christmas, "It's almost time! Is everyone excited?"

Rolling my eyes, I say in a monotone, "Yeah, Miss G." Miss G hears the sarcasm and frowns. A couple of my classmates in the front row turn, give me a dirty look, and start clapping. Miss G smiles. GATE kids are such kiss-asses. I'm over it. I have my black Siouxsie Sioux eyeliner on thick, and my eyes stare down everyone. I have already begun my metamorphosis from goody-two-shoes to punk-rock girl. By the following year, the change will be complete and my nose will be pierced and I will be ditching every class in my red combat monkey boots.

The Challenger space shuttle liftoff is live on TV today. Miss G has been excited about this for weeks. She says it is especially inspirational because a teacher is on board the shuttle. Miss G is young. She looks more like an older sister than a teacher, with pale skin and short black hair and wide brown eyes. Her cheeks are always pink. She wears cute dresses and colorful cardigans with pearls, and her hair flips up like Mary Tyler Moore. Miss G is always very encouraging. She says I am a good writer.

Miss G is wandering around getting everything set up. I tap my feet and sneak my headphones on under my hooded sweatshirt. I press play and Morrissey's yearning voice wails in my ears. I close my eyes and sway in my seat.

My friend Rose, who loves music like I do, nudges me. I put my headphones around my neck—I can still hear Morrissey's voice—and she says, "What's on the tape?"

"The Smiths' first album," I murmur back. Rose gives me a thumbs-up.

I put the headphones back on and turn the volume up. The jangling chords of Johnny Marr's guitar on "This Charming Man" ring in my ears. I can't help myself and start tapping my feet. Hearing the tapping, Miss G, who has bionic ears and eagle eyes, turns around from adjusting the antenna on the television and says in her stern voice, "Juanita, Walkman off. Now!"

My friend Jim, a blond-haired swim-team god who I have a crush on, turns and smiles my way. He winks at me, his sky-blue eyes crinkling. My heart beats fast and I can feel my cheeks turning red. I don't wink back. It's not as if he could pick me up on a date at my house because he would have to meet the crazies.

I shrug at Miss G, throw the Walkman into my backpack, and pull out *Wifey*. I had covered it with a brown paper bag and decorated it with the names of my favorite bands, The Smiths and The Cure, in cursive purple ink. I fall right back into the story where I left off. I guess I don't know why the main character Sandy Pressman ever got married. Marriage seems like such a shit-show. Just ask my parents.

Miss G yells in a giddy voice, "It's almost time!"

I whisper "Yeahhhhhhh" under my breath and roll my eyes.

With a slam, I close my book and the entire class watches the television in silence. No one says a word. The images on the television are a bit blurry, but squinting, I can see the hazy image of the shuttle and the flames shooting out from under it. Waiting for takeoff.

We all listen to the announcer on live TV.

They are lucky to get away into space, far away from here. It must be peaceful out there floating in the universe. Quiet would be nice. I imagine myself on the shuttle, in an ivory spacesuit and helmet, strapped down, ready to take off. I bet it wouldn't even get boring out there in space. They probably let you bring a lot of books to read.

The countdown begins and, as if we are in church, we all lean forward, hands clasped. "T minus fifteen seconds. T minus ten. Nine, eight, seven, six, five, four, three, two, one."

David Bowie's song "Space Oddity" plays in my head".

"And liftoff."

The shuttle takes off into the air slowly. It must weigh a ton. We watch, our chins rising in unison as the shuttle lifts off almost as if it is pulled by some unseen force. Miss G grins and then all us kids look at one another and then back to the television, marveling at it all.

"Isn't it beautiful? What a miracle," Miss G says in a soft, velvet-blanket kind of voice, like she is looking at the Sistine Chapel. She is in awe.

Orange flames soar underneath the shuttle and the shuttle lifts even higher, up into the sky with a tail trailing behind it. The class cheers.

***

Moments later, almost like a balloon popping unexpectedly, it happens. Everyone shrieks. Awe turns to horror as something explodes into shiny pieces on the television. On the screen, I see thick curls of smoke in the sky. Squinting, I shake my head and my throat feels as if it is swelling.

"What happened?" a couple of the kids say. "Where's the shuttle?"

The screen is so tiny and blurry from where I am in the back row. I am trying to see, but all I see on the screen is smoke and more smoke. The announcer seems confused. He is talking about the boosters and then he says that there has been a major malfunction.

I think of David Bowie's lyrics, the ones calling out for Major Tom.

More minutes go by, and the announcer finally says what we are starting to figure out, "The vessel has exploded."

This can't be true, I think. *Exploded? It's gone? They're all gone?*

I imagine myself inside the shuttle with flames burning my suit, my face melting, and my skin turning to gray ash. It burns, it burns. Fade to black. I remember the time Jackie lit the living room on fire. We were little and I stood still as a statue for a moment, mesmerized by the flames running up the curtains, until I grabbed the hose from outside and put the fire out. No one can put this fire out. Maybe staying on Earth is a good idea.

We all stare at Miss G. Miss G is weeping, big tears running down her face. She sobs the word "no" over and over, almost like a prayer, "No. No. No. Please no."

My own eyes well up and my face feels hot. I wipe my face on my sleeve and see black streaks of liner. I put my arms on my desk and rest my head, one eye peeking out beneath my hood.

My classmates start to whimper, and then, everyone is crying. I am weeping, too, despite myself. I thought I couldn't cry anymore, that I was done crying. This feels different, as if the entire planet is sobbing at once.

Miss G walks up and turns the television off.

I can't stop more tears from falling. They fall and fall, and I think *Why is life always like this? Life sucks. A beautiful day turned to shit so quickly. The Challenger story should have had a happy ending.*

***

Later that night, I am in my bedroom, on my bed, with a pillow over my ears trying to muffle the sounds of my parents fighting. The screaming is so loud that it feels as if I'm living in that movie with Jack Nicholson and Danny DeVito. My very own cuckoo's nest. I go to the bathroom and make myself throw up. I feel better after, like something was released. I turn on my record player. I play my favorite Smiths album, *Meat is Murder*, and hum along to the calming lull of Morrissey's voice.

Mom and Dad didn't even ask me about the liftoff. They were too busy arguing and cursing and throwing plates at one other. All I keep thinking is that I want a place of my own when I grow up. Somewhere beautiful and quiet, like outer space.

Silver Spoons

I was born with a plastic spoon in my mouth, the pink kind you get at Dairy Queen. There were no silver spoons in my house. Mom waitressed and Dad was a truck driver who loved his beer, and he loved it even more once he bought his bar.

Just like Mom said (she is right about a lot about things), a drinker owning a bar is a disaster waiting to happen. Soon, as one would expect, the bar went belly-up and, like something out of a Dickens novel, so did my parents' finances. They had mortgaged the house to buy the bar. In a sign of defeat, Mom and Dad filed bankruptcy and let our house go.

Life changed when they lost the house. Mom was furious with Dad. She ranted and raved. "It's all your father's fault," she muttered in a bitter voice. "I should have never signed those damn loan papers."

We were forced to rent. Mom found a deal on a three-bedroom condominium in Upland, a city just north of

Ontario.

If Ontario was a Budweiser-like town, Upland was a Champagne-type city, although anything below Foothill was considered less desirable. The condo was on D Street and Euclid, right below Foothill, and within walking distance of Chaffey High School.

Mom and Dad had fought hard and loud in the Ontario house. Annie worried about moving to the condo because we shared a wall with our next-door neighbors. Mom and Dad pledged that it would be different, but as quick as Mom could scream "Fucking asshole!" we were once again the talk of the neighborhood. I didn't care because it was my sophomore year of high school and I spent most of my time hanging out with my new best friend Tracy.

Tracy and I met in Chaffey's "YOU" class in 1986. The "YOU" class was a cross between a psychology and sociology course. Tracy sat a couple of seats behind me and I admired her style from the first day. Tracy had light blonde hair with spiked-up bangs, and she wore red lipstick and thick black eyeliner around her eyes like Siouxsie. I felt like I wasn't cool enough to talk to her because she hung out with Mariella, a popular cheerleader who looked like Nia Peeples.

One day after class, Tracy came up to me and started talking as if she knew me. She thought I was my twin Jackie, who she had PE with. We started talking about music and it turned out that we were both obsessed with The Smiths. We had an instant connection, the kind that usually only happens in the movies. I wanted to be just like her.

I remember the first time we hung out together. Her mom picked me up in front of the condo in a blue Chevy

Blazer. When they drove up, Tracy's mom asked if my mom wanted to meet her and I waved off the question. The day at Corona Del Mar was a dream. Tracy's mom didn't yell at any drivers on the road. We soaked up the sun all day and grabbed lunch. I didn't want to go home that night.

A couple of weekends later, Tracy's mom took us to Hollywood, where we went to Nana's on Melrose and I bought red monkey boots, a short version of a combat boot. The next weekend, we went to Claremont and hung out at the Crystal Cave. Tracy bought a pentacle on a long velvet string and I bought a necklace with an Egyptian cross symbol. We spent hours reading books about astrological signs and tarot cards.

Although it made me nervous, I introduced Tracy to my mom. My other best friend Melinda always handled Mom's variations of moods with ease. Melinda never held it against me if Mom told her to "Get the fuck out." I wondered if Tracy would be understanding about what it was like in my house.

There was no need to worry because Tracy handled it like a trooper and Mom's affection for Tracy surprised me. Tracy always smiled at Mom when she came home tired from work, and made conversation. When Mom got angry, Tracy would just say with laughter in her voice, "Your mom's fucking crazy." We would go to my room, crank up some Smiths or Pixies, and make fun of Mom's expressions.

Later that year, my family received an invitation to my cousin Queytay's wedding in Orange County. Queytay was the daughter of Uncle Poncho and Aunt Tilly. Dad hated Tilly and didn't want to go, but Mom said he had to go even though he complained that Mom's brothers talked about him in Spanish.

Mom said I could bring Tracy and we picked her up in Dad's beat-up old pickup. My sisters and I opened up the back to the shell and waved Tracy inside. Mom and Dad bickered the whole way to Orange County. Tracy and I giggled in the back of the truck while my parents cussed each other out.

Tracy had dyed her hair pink for the wedding with cherry Kool Aid. My hair was short and curly. We had colored it blue-black the weekend before. I borrowed Tracy's red lipstick, which matched my monkey boots, and Tracy applied my eyeliner so it looked like hers. We wore similar outfits of concert T-shirts and black skirts with black tights. Jackie wore a tight dress and, when she saw Tracy and me standing side by side, she looked at us askance and said, "Are you guys really wearing that?"

When we got to the reception we grabbed a table and Mom and Dad took Annie and went to talk to the relatives. We noticed the bartender was a preppy twenty-something guy with sandy hair. Jackie sauntered over to him and struck up a conversation. She motioned us over and he handed us a small plastic glass with a yellow liquid inside and whispered, "Kamikaze."

Tracy and I went to the alley behind the recreation room to do our shots. We drank the kamikazes quickly and grimaced with the tang of vodka and lemon. There were a number of guys hanging out back there, some in their teens and some older.

Jackie hung out at the bar talking to the bartender and

his friend who was the deejay. Tracy and I smoked cigarettes outside, and we did a round of purple shots that tasted like grape punch.

Soon, my head was spinning. We were out of cigarettes. I walked into the recreation room and saw Mom's purse sitting on a chair. Looking around, I grabbed the keys and walked up to the bar where Tracy and Jackie were joking with the bartender. "Let's go," I said to Tracy. "We need cigs."

"You stay in case Mom and Dad are looking for us," I ordered Jackie, who nodded her head in agreement.

I nominated Tracy to drive. Tracy was always a worrier, but I convinced her that everything would be fine. She had a hard time maneuvering the bulky pickup through the complex. We drove down the street looking for a gas station, and I told her to "flip a bitch" when I saw a 7-Eleven.

As Tracy made the U-turn, a car headed straight for us and I screamed. Tracy swerved the truck, barely avoiding an accident. We pulled into the parking lot of the 7-Eleven and looked at each other, and Tracy said in a shaky voice, "That was close, Waa-Waa." Tracy always calls me Waa-Waa, short for Juanita, my real name.

I found a guy to buy us cigarettes and then we drove back. We must have turned the wrong way because we made our way through a maze of streets before we found the apartment complex. Mom and Dad met us at the front door of the recreation room and Mom grabbed the keys out of my hand. We were caught.

"We were just listening to music, Mom," I said. She shook her head and said, "Where the fuck is Jackie?"

My uncle Poncho and Aunt Tilly walked over and asked if anything was wrong. "Judy, calm down," Dad said with a slur in his voice. I stammered, "I'll go get her." Tracy's eyes begged me to hurry.

I found Jackie and told her, "C'mon, Mom and Dad are pissed." We followed Mom and Dad to the pickup truck. Dad could barely walk. Mom was screaming at him. We all piled in as he started the truck. The truck refused to budge.

"John, you're just fucking drunk, that's the problem," Mom screamed.

Dad threw his hands up in the air and said with resignation, "Judy, I can't get the car to go." Mom's brother Roland drove us home that night in his van (we found out later that "someone" had left the emergency brake on). The drive home seemed interminable. Mom yelled at us the whole way. I placed my face against the window and watched the cities roll by on the 57 freeway.

When we got home, Mom said, "You girls need to go to bed. You are going to school tomorrow, don't even think about trying to stay home."

Tracy and I sat cross-legged on my bed and talked for an hour before we turned out the lights and went to sleep.

In the morning, Mom woke us up with a yell. "Get up, you're late!" she screamed.

To get Mom off our backs, we all got dressed and walked down Euclid toward school like a trio of misfits.

We knew Mom had to leave soon for her breakfast shift. We walked for about half an hour and when we were about five or six blocks away from school, Tracy looked at me and said, "You think she's gone yet?" Jackie and I nodded in unison and we turned around and walked back to the condo.

Thankfully, Mom had already left. Jackie went to bed and Tracy and I parked ourselves on the couch and watched *Alice, Sweet Alice,* a creepy slasher movie starring Brooke Shields.

We took turns dipping into Dad's container of Thrifty's ice cream with our plastic spoons.

Besties

As you know, I have two best friends, Melinda and Tracy. I have known Melinda since I was a little girl. We have been riding our bicycles through the suburban streets for most of my childhood. Our friendship and history together are part of who I am. We have crazy adventures, too many to count. There is the time we get drunk at a friend's house in junior high and walk home in the rain. Somehow, Melinda comes home, dripping wet, with only one shoe on. We are both put on restriction.

Growing up, I want to be Melinda. In junior high, I covet her straight black spiky hair and her cool jean jackets with concert buttons lined up on the right side, and her sarcastic glances and sayings. "Stop smiling," she always tells me. "You look like a geek."

Plus, she understands my family. Mom goes from nice to shrieking in a minute and Melinda always just weathers it and ignores it. We even giggle about it later.

Now we're in high school, and she is even better looking. It's so not fair. She looks like a Mexican version of the lead singer of the Bangles. I could never compete with her. She is a total guy magnet.

We are getting ready to go to the junior prom tonight. Melinda is trying to help me with my makeup and hair, to no avail. She is trying to straighten my hair and I am starting to look like a puffy poodle. To make matters worse, the red dress I am wearing looked good in the window, but its shiny apple color doesn't suit my skin. Melinda looks amazing in a tight, iridescent lavender dress that she bought at the Gunne Sax outlet, especially paired with her purple eyeshadow.

Melinda looks at me and raises an eyebrow. "Why does your hair get so frizzy?" She says it with a sarcastic grin, so I smile back with crooked teeth and say equally sarcastically, "Because you fucked it up."

To make matters worse than just frizzy hair, Melinda has set me up with her boyfriend Todd's friend so we can double date for prom. I had anticipated being set up with Julian, one of his handsome punker friends, but the guy who comes with Todd to Melinda's door that night is about five-foot-three with long, Jesus-like hair and a mustache.

"What happened to Julian, the cute tall guy?" I whisper to Melinda. "Something came up," she says with a shrug. I know she doesn't want to hurt my feelings, so I just shrug and say, "Whatever."

They take us to Cask and Cleaver and, eternal optimist that I am, I try to make the best of it. The Jesus lookalike doesn't say a word, and the less he says, the more I babble. When we finally get to the dance, I try to dance with him, but he keeps counting in my ear.

Thankfully, like so many times I have with Melinda, things end abruptly. Todd gets caught drinking, and we all get kicked out of the dance. That puts an end to the guy with Jesus-like hair.

Our favorite activity in high-school was ditching. When my mom dropped us off, Jackie and I ran and grabbed Melinda and maneuvered ourselves off campus by car or bus. We walked to Montclair Plaza and begged for quarters. "Could we please have a quarter?" one of us would say in a sweet voice. "We need to call our mom to pick us up."

Picture this. Melinda has spiked black hair and is wearing her typical attire of ripped jeans and a tight blouse. I have thick black Siouxsie eyeliner on. I am wearing a concert tee with thermals covered by men's boxers and combat boots. Jackie has blonde bangs and is probably wearing some type of lace dress. Suffice to say, Jackie and Melinda usually do the asking. I would not have given us a dime, but people do.

We earn a little or a lot of dough depending on how crowded the mall is. Sometimes, we accidentally ask the same people twice and they look at us with a scowl, sensing a scam. With our stash, we share fast food in the mall's food court.

After eating, we stand out in the front of the mall and chain-smoke. We buy our cigarettes at the liquor store next door to Melinda's duplex with a note signed by my mom (aka, my handwriting). We smoke Marlboro Lights. I first started smoking in elementary school when a girl named Christy asked me to come to her house after school. She lived in the Section Eight apartments across the street. We stole a pack of her mom's Virginia Slims from the freezer. Christy taught me how to smoke in the park behind the restrooms. I only coughed a little.

Back to the ditching. One day, Melinda and I ditched without Jackie, and we drove to Hollywood in Melinda's 1964 white Corvair. We had heard a rumor that the new Oingo Boingo album was going on sale at Tower Records.

When we arrived at the record store, we noticed some commotion and realized that the band was there. I shook hands with the lead singer Danny Elfman, while Melinda chatted with Johnny Vatos the drummer. We screamed the whole way home.

When we got back late that afternoon, I raved to Jackie about meeting Oingo Boingo and she yelled with tears in her eyes, "Oingo is my favorite band, not yours!"

Melinda and I would go to Newport every week, blasting the Violent Femmes in her Corvair. We went to a punk store called Electric Chair and I got my nose pierced. I had a seizure and hit my head on the glass countertop. It didn't matter. I felt like the coolest girl in the world when I went to school with the little diamond stud in my nose. There was only one other girl at school who had her nose pierced. Mom threw a fit and slapped me in the face when she saw the nose piercing. It was worth the slap.

Our other favorite pastime was crank calling. We flipped through the phone book and picked a random number to call. When someone answered, we asked, "Is your refrigerator running? Yes? Then go catch it." The joke was old and stale but it never got old to us. Elderly people's reactions were always the funniest.

My other bestie was Tracy, and we had a special connection. She could always make me laugh harder than anyone I ever knew. We were both obsessed with music and would listen to all of our favorite bands on repeat—the Smiths, Generation X, the Buzzcocks, Sisters of Mercy, the Pixies, The Replacements, X, The Cure, Echo and the Bunnymen, The Cult, and others. We would spend Saturdays listening to music, blasting the radio on KROQ, and dancing our hearts out.

Tracy and I would make ham sandwiches at her house with the thin, processed ham her mom bought, on white bread with mayo and Ruffles. Soon, we figured out a way to get free food by calling restaurants to complain. For some reason, we always used an English accent. Tracy would call McDonald's and say in her best British voice, "I just bought some food and found a hair in my Big Mac." Typically, the manager would get on the phone and say, "Please accept our apologies and pick up food on us."

I remember one time we picked up our food. I was wearing my mom's fake fur, high heels, and huge sunglasses. Tracy had on a raincoat and combat boots. I suppose we thought we were incognito, but the reality was that we just didn't care what people thought. We still don't.

Tracy and I worked at Round Table and worked the delivery phones in the back room. Our friends would drive to the back door for free pizza. At night, if the "cool" manager Jeff was on duty, we would stay after work late and drink free beer. We would play music and laugh and talk, play Pac-Man, down Coors Light like it was water, and smoke cigarette after cigarette in the back parking lot.

What I remember most about that junior year of high school were the concerts, too many to count. We used our paychecks to see every band we could. I saw so many bands live, including The Smiths, The Cure, Peter Murphy, Siouxsie, The Pixies, X, The Church, the Violent Femmes, and one of my favorite bands, The Replacements, along with lesser-known bands like Dramarama.

That was before everything went to shit.

Stay Gold

Mom's at work so Dad's downstairs in the condo we live in listening to country music and drinking all the beer he wants. He's been drinking even more Budweiser since he lost the house and his bar. Mom says he's happy as a pig in shit when he drinks.

Dad's only income is from his disability payments, so Mom's working two jobs to pay the bills. She works the night shift at Yahtzee's Chinese restaurant and a couple of graveyard shifts at Circle K. She's always so tired and angry. There are days I feel bad for her but then she treats me like shit and I hate her all over again.

I hear Dad yell in a slurry voice, "I'll be back, Jenny, I need cigarettes."

The front door slams with a thud. I run outside and yell, "Dad, wait!" to see if I can stop him.

Dad's blue-and-white Dodge pickup truck is already puttering down the street. He waves out his window at me. It's almost dusk and I watch the setting sun throw gold into the clouds.

Dad's probably going to a bar.

Before Mom had left for work, they got into another

fight. Their same fight is on repeat like my favorite Smiths albums. Mom had screamed at him, "John, it's all your fucking fault we lost the house and have to live in this damn rental. My brothers always told me that my borracho gringo husband would put me in the poorhouse one day. They were right. I should never have married you."

Dad had muttered his usual response from his La-Z-Boy recliner as he watched TV. "Judy, you know you let me buy that bar."

"Fuck you, John," Mom said, and left for work in a huff, but not before throwing her coffee cup at his head. She missed. After all these years together, Dad has learned to duck. We all have.

It's so quiet. Annie is at her best friend's house and Jackie is out with her friends. I change the station from Dad's hillbilly one to KROQ. The Sex Pistols are playing and I jump up and down to the beat.

Tapping my feet, I hum along to the next song on KROQ, "White Girl," by one of my favorite punk bands, X. People call me white girl all the time because my dad is white. I always say, "I am not a white girl, I am brown and Mexican, like my mom."

Maybe I don't fit in anywhere.

My hand shakes as I put on my bright red lipstick in the bathroom, squinting at the mirror. Next, I draw on my upper lids with thick black eyeliner, making pointed edges mimicking Siouxsie Sioux's eyeliner. My lines are crooked, but it's the best I can do.

Grabbing one of Dad's beers out of the fridge, I down it and throw it in the trash, making sure to wipe the lipstick off. Dad will never remember how many he had.

Tonight, I am going out to a club with my two best friends, Tracy and Melinda. We are going to Marilyn's in Pasadena, a sixteen-and-over dance club that caters to alternatives. They play all our favorite bands: The Smiths, The Cure, Siouxsie and the Banshees, Echo and the Bunnymen, and Joy Division.

I am a below-the-track kind of kid now. It wasn't always this way. We lost everything when Dad's bar was taken by the bank. They took the house next, and now we move from rental to rental. I used to be a preppie, straight-A student who wanted to go to Claremont McKenna College. Now, I'm ditching or sleeping through class and drinking all the time, becoming a ghost of a girl.

Some days, I feel like a character from one of my favorite books, *The Outsiders*. There is a scene where all the Greasers and Socs fight in the park to let loose their rage. My favorite character is the narrator, Ponyboy. He's a dreamer, and his favorite poem is "Nothing Gold Can Stay" by Robert Frost. That's the theme of *The Outsiders*: No one can stay pure for very long, but you have to try to stay innocent, meaning gold.

All the kids in my GATE classes call me a witch because my nose is pierced and I wear an ankh necklace and dress in concert tees, along with my red monkey boots from Nana's on Melrose.

I don't care what the kids at school think. They're just mad that the Econ teacher gave me an A in class even though I ditch every other class to go to Hollywood. He said I aced the essays.

School is easy. Life is hard.

Tonight, I am wearing a tight black skull dress and tights that I ripped up myself, with a pair of black leather boots with skull buckles up the side. My box-bought blue-black hair is in ringlets.

It gets later and later, and still no Dad. I picture him still at the bar, on a stool, waving his glass in the air. Dad knows Mom will be home late from her shift at the restaurant. I write him a note on a paper towel in black marker. "Going out, be home late. Love, Jenny." I draw a little heart at the bottom.

I go outside to smoke a cigarette and wait. I blow smoke rings and practice my French inhale. Tracy picks me up in her red Honda Civic with a "beep beep" of her horn. I smile big and wide and wave her to the curb, holding a bottle of Strawberry Hill that an older kid down the street scored for me.

For the first time in a while, I feel happy and free. All I have on my mind tonight is going out and drinking. I want to get fucked up.

Melinda is in the back seat. She has her black hair spiked up and she is wearing a tight black dress with a silver dagger on it and a green army jacket. Tracy is wearing a black lace dress, and her platinum-dyed blonde hair is sticking straight up in the front. Her green eyes are lined like Siouxsie too, but her lines are straight and dramatic, unlike mine.

"Hey, Waa-Waa" Tracy says.

"Hey, Tray-Tray," I say in a sing-song voice back.

Melinda takes a chug from a beer. "Hey, Mel," I say. "Are we gonna dance tonight?"

Melinda shrugs her shoulders, in her usual sarcastic-girl way, and with a smiling grimace says, "If we drink enough." We've been friends so long that I can tell when Melinda has had a bad day and wants to get drunk. Her dad is from Mexico and stern and super strict.

"We will paarrrty," I say, laughing. Melinda and I do a high five. I light up a cigarette and blow the smoke out the window as Tracy takes off. It always relaxes me to smoke. Mom and Dad and all of their problems fall away in the haze of Marlboro Lights.

There is an unspoken agreement that I always get the front seat no matter who drives. Maybe it is because I am best friends with Melinda and Tracy but they are not best friends with one another. When we are all together, I feel at peace. We never fight and we always have good times.

Tracy's little Civic is a compact, one of the tiny, bug-looking cars. Her back windshield is covered with stickers for Black Flag, The Cure, and The Misfits.

We blast music all the way to Pasadena. I swig from the bottle of wine as Tracy drives. I need to be buzzed by the time we get to the club so I can dance. The wine relaxes me even more than the cigarette did.

"Be careful, Waa-Waa," Tracy scolds, glancing at her rear-view mirror. "Watch out for the reit-reits."

Reit-reits means piggies, which means cops. I grab a 7-Eleven plastic cup from the floor and pour some of the Strawberry Hill in and hand it over. Tracy downs it with a gulp while watching the road, one hand on the wheel. Melinda's given up the beer. She says she doesn't want to look bloated, and takes sips from the bottle of tequila she stole from her parent's liquor cabinet.

The three of us sing in unison to the Violent Femmes song "Blister in the Sun" that plays on the tape deck.

Tracy parks the car. We stay in the car to finish our drinks, and watch the throngs of boys with mohawks and girls with purple hair and pierced noses. I drink every drop of the wine. I feel dizzy but elated. Tracy and I finish Melinda's beer and I do a shot of tequila for good measure. "Cheers, bitches," Melinda squeals as we finish off the bottle.

We walk up to the club and I see a Matt Dillon lookalike in Levi's and rolled-up sleeves lounging outside the club, smoking. I swoon inside and whisper to Tracy, "He looks just like Dallas from The Outsiders."

Tracy whispers back, "You should go up and talk to him. You look great tonight and he'll be impressed by how smart you are." I shake my head and walk on by.

We get in line. It's fifty people long, and Melinda stands by the front of the line and winks at the bouncer. Boys love Melinda, who looks like a Mexican version of Susanna Hoffs from the Bangles. Just like Susanna, Melinda is thin with straight, dark spiky hair and wide eyes. The bouncer keeps checking Melinda out and finally, after ten minutes, he waves us to the front of the line.

It's loud in the club. A Depeche Mode song is on and the electronic dance beats of "I Just Can't Get Enough" fill the air. The music takes over me; the thud of the beat erases my cares. We run in and dance in a circle to "This Corrosion" by Sisters of Mercy. Tones on Tail's song "Go!" comes on next, and we scream as we raise our hands in the hair and jump up and down. I feel alive in a way I don't when I'm at school. I dance and lose myself in the music. My eyes well up when I think of home, but I sway until the thoughts disappear.

A girl bumps into me and I smile. Melinda looks at her and says, "Bitch." I yank Melinda away and point out a cute punker guy with white hair, a Billy Idol lookalike, for Melinda to hook up with. Soon, she is making out with him at a corner table.

Tracy and I walk around the club and finally get the nerve to ask the deejay to play The Smiths. He obliges and we dance to "Ask." I fall into a trance listening to Morrissey's sweet and aching voice. I feel my eyes start to water and shake my head.

Two boys in all black with big messy hair and eyeliner ask us to dance.

They are trying hard, maybe too hard, to look like Robert Smith.

Tracy and I do our dance where we wave our hands in the air to the music. We talk in fake English accents, laughing, and pretend to be robots. The boys walk away.

We giggle, both buzzed, link arms, and dance in circles. "Besties and witches forever," we chant.

Two phrases repeat in my head: This is joy. This is life.

Melinda takes a break from making out with fake Billy Idol to walk over to us. She raises an eyebrow, which I take to mean "Stop being dorks." We are having too much fun, so I laugh and wave away her judgment.

Tracy, Melinda, and I dance in a circle to Siouxsie and the Banshee's "Cities in Dust." My head spins from the music and the alcohol and the colors from the strobes that flash in my eyes. I feel as if I could dance forever.

The club closes a little after two a.m. and we mingle in the parking lot, smoking and talking to people.

On the ride back home, I keep Tracy awake. The alcohol is wearing off and the euphoria of the night is giving way to dread about going home.

After dropping Melinda off, Tracy pulls up to my house and asks me in a worried voice, "Are you gonna be OK? You can come to my house if you need to." I shake my head, but I can feel my heart racing. "I'm good, bestie. Thanks though," I say, giving Tracy a half-hug. I watch her pull away and steel my shoulders.

I stumble inside. Dad is asleep on his recliner. Mom is in the doorway, still dressed in her red waitress uniform.

Mom is angry. "Where have you been?" she says. She has that look in her eyes. She screams, "Do you want to be a pendeja loser? You've been ditching school again! Your teacher came into the restaurant and told me you missed two-thirds of your classes."

I shake my head at her and mutter, "I'm tired. Leave me the hell alone."

Mom keeps yelling at me saying that I am going to ruin my life. She says that I look ridiculous, and that I am a fuck-up. I know I am a fuck-up, a loser, but I can't help it. I don't care about anything anymore.

What Mom doesn't understand, and will never understand, is that if life means working and fighting and hating each other and then waking up every day to do it again, I don't want any of it. I just want to dance and listen to music and have fun.

If a "life" is what my parents have, I would rather be

dead.

Closing my eyes, still a little drunk, I sway and think to myself, "Stay gold, Ponyboy." Mom continues to rant and rave. I feel her hands hit my back but it doesn't hurt. Maybe they used to hurt when I was little. Now, I don't feel anything at all.

Is this what growing up is supposed to feel like?

One thing I know for sure is that I am an Outsider. But fuck staying gold. I am already black and blue.

Soda Pop Bottles

We get evicted from the condo.

Part of it was my fault. I am one of the holy terrors of the neighborhood. I make out with a boy in the community jacuzzi, beer bottle in hand. I steal my dad's car at night and come home to red-and-blue lights flashing in our driveway. I toilet-paper Downtown Upland, which turns into a criminal investigation after a friend vandalizes a car with permanent marker. I get caught by the cops drinking in the front yard with my skater boyfriend and his stoner friends and am almost arrested, but instead they cite me. As my penance I attend alcohol classes, where they tell me to "Just say no." Add in Mom and Dad's constant screaming and fighting and, in essence, they evict my family for being modern-day Inland Empire troublemakers and hillbillies.

Mom and Dad rush to find another rental. It isn't easy. The manager of the condos in Upland dislikes our family due to our proclivity for fighting and throwing things, and refused to give us a good reference.

I was glad to leave the condos. I had relationship drama. My short-lived crush on my seventeen-year-old neighbor Hovie came to a bitter end after he took up with my neighbor Cathy, who went to Claremont High. Cathy was pretty in a quirky, Ally Sheedy kind of way and loved the Grateful Dead. I winced every time they drove by in Hovie's convertible MG.

Christian is next. He is a skateboarder with curly brown hair and freckles who smokes pot all day instead of going to school. Christian gives me a diamond stud earring that I return when he dumps me for a girl who was more willing and open with her affections.

Mom stresses out about finding another rental, but she finally found a two-story house in Upland. The house is old and looks like a large white castle with peeling paint. It has four bedrooms, two baths, and about twenty windows. It sits on a huge lot surrounded by old trees, just east of Euclid and Arrow.

The house scares me a bit. It is always so cold. The TV room has a sloping roof that meets up in a V, and the ceiling is so low that you have to bend to enter. When she spends the night, Tracy and I use the Ouija board in the room and the disc moves on its own. From then on, we are convinced that the TV room is haunted.

My sisters and I are still paying my parents back for all the chaos we had endured as kids. I ditch school whenever possible, and I spend my weekends drinking and carousing with Tracy and Melinda.

On one such "ditch" day, Melinda and I drive to Hollywood to visit a punk-rock store. I buy some red creepers with zebra-fur detailing. The radio in Melinda's car is broken, so we drive home from Hollywood blasting the Violent Femmes in a boom box on my lap.

After Melinda drops me off, I walk inside, creepers in hand, and shout out, "Jackie, look what I bought in Hollywood today." Mom comes out from the kitchen and slaps me and screams, "Goddammit, Jenny, you need to stop ditching." I run to my room, shut the door, and caress my shoes as I hum the Violent Femmes song "Kiss Off."

We steal my dad's truck and drive through the tree-lined streets of Upland, hooting and hollering at the other cars. When we stop at a red light, we wave our hands in the air and change seats.

One night, Annie and her friend Pam walk into my bedroom after midnight dressed like cat burglars, in dark sweats with black ski hats on their heads. Pam puts her finger against her lips and whispers, "Are you ready?" I nod and we tiptoe into the living room, where my dad snores on the couch in his pajama pants and white T-shirt.

I look in on Mom. There are peanut butter cracker crumbs all over her bedspread and her book is on the floor. We wait fifteen minutes to make sure she is asleep and then I creep into the living room on all fours and pull the keys out of Dad's Wranglers.

Pam wants to drive. Even though she is only fourteen, she is the best driver of all of us because her dad taught her how to drive his car when she was twelve. Pam jumps into the driver's seat on top of a phone book so she can reach the steering wheel. Annie sits in the middle of the bench seat and I sit against the window. The car smells like stale cigarettes. We start the truck and Pam backs it out of the driveway with the lights off.

We drive up and down Euclid Avenue for about fifteen

minutes. We blast the radio on Power 106, and Pam and Annie get on my dad's CB intercom and cuss out cars in Spanish. As we turn down Ninth Street, the truck starts to sputter. Pam pulls over. I lean over and look at the gas gauge. Empty. We are out of gas. I look at Annie, Annie looks at Pam, and Pam looks at me and says, "Come on, let's go get some gas before your parents wake up and freak out."

We run home as fast as we can, taking the side streets, and get back to the house out of breath. Dad is still asleep. Annie runs upstairs to her room to get money out of her piggy bank. Jackie walks into the living room rubbing her eyes. "What are you guys doing?" Jackie says.

I point at Dad and motion her into the kitchen. "We took Dad's truck and we ran out of gas," I tell her in a low, matter-of-fact voice. Jackie makes a face and says, "Why didn't you wake me up?"

Pam rifles through the kitchen and holds up four empty plastic two-liters of Diet Rite and says, "These will do." We each grab one and set off to the gas station, including Jackie, who has her winter coat on over her pajamas.

We sprint down Arrow Highway, bottles in hand, and hide behind trees whenever we see headlights. We turn down Campus to Ninth Street and race each other back to the gas station. Pam hands the gas station cashier a couple of dollars.

"Put it all on number four," Pam says with a wink. The cashier glances at us with a skeptical look and shakes her head but punches it into the register. Pam stands in front of us as we place the nozzle inside the bottles and fill them each about three-quarters full. We run down the street just as the clerk storms out of the gas station door screaming, "You stupid kids, you're supposed to get a gas can. I'm calling the police."

We flip her off and run up Ninth Street as if the devil himself was chasing us. We know if the cops come we are busted. When we get back to the truck, we tilt the soda bottles into the tank one by one and jump in the truck as Pam pumps the gas. We all cheer as the engine roars back to life and drive home.

Mom and Dad don't catch us that night and we keep on taking the truck out, but we make sure the gas tank is full.

Later that year, the owners of the creepy Upland house tell us that they are selling. My sisters and I groan with displeasure when we find out we have to move again.

We are back in Ontario in yet another rental for my senior year of high school. That year is going to be a doozy.

Kegger

The idea for a kegger party came to me during my last year of high school. It started out as only an idea and the idea became reality. Then, as it often did in my childhood, reality turned ugly.

By this time, we lived off 4th Street in a small three-bedroom rental. When we moved to the new, not-so-new rental, I claimed my own room as the oldest twin by Biblical birthright. Jackie was forced to share a room with Annie.

I loved the privacy. I had a poster of Sid Vicious on one wall (I blew a kiss to him every morning) and a poster of Bono from U2 on the other. I romanticized Sid. Tracy and I would watch the movie *Sid and Nancy* over and over. To us, they were like Romeo and Juliet, only a punk-rock version.

My cat Whitey was a permanent fixture on my bed, and she always left white hair on my all-black wardrobe. I had my nose pierced and proudly wore my diamond stud to school. It got me a lot of attention. I even had a boyfriend, a guy named Kenny who had a mohawk. Tracy and I attended homecoming by double-dating with our boyfriends Kenny and Ken. My boyfriend Kenny wore a shiny silver suit that coordinated well with the color of his mohawk. Tracy's boyfriend Ken wore a top hat with his tuxedo-like suit and suspenders. He carried a cane like the guy in *A Clockwork Orange*.

After the dance, I found out my parents were going away. "No parties," Dad said with a wag of his finger when Mom told us they were leaving for Laughlin that weekend. Annie (aka, the narc) was going to stay with her friend Bernadette. "Party—no way!" I guffawed with a flourish of my hand, and the idea was born. I called Tracy that night to start the planning.

Keg parties were all the rage in the Inland Empire of the nineteen-eighties. The recipe was a simple mix of beer and high-school students. Add in a band or at the very least a boom box and the recipe was complete.

We started party planning at Round Table in Upland, a pizza place where Tracy and I worked most nights. Melinda stopped by after her shift at the mall and we worked out all the details.

I decided to "borrow" a couple of kegs from the cooler at Round Table and have them filled by a co-worker's older brother. "We need fliers to pass out at school," I said as the unofficial president of the planning committee. "Johnny can draw; let's have him hand-sketch one and we can make copies. Have him put in some skulls and beer bottles," Tracy said. Melinda joined in, "Yeah, and let's charge three bucks a head." We made a hundred fliers and passed them out all week at lunch.

The day of the party, Tracy and I talked about it in our area of the punker quad where we hung out. Melinda walked toward us with a grimace. "Guess who else is having a party tonight? Reggie."

"Shit, we're screwed," I muttered back. "When the football king has a party, everyone goes."

That night, I waited at the house, drinking out of the keg with Tracy, Melinda, and the two guys we hired to work the door. By nine we had given up. No one was coming. All of a sudden, we heard shouting and screaming coming from the front of the house. I walked into the front yard and saw at least twenty cars parked on the street.

A guy in a football jersey walked up and said, "Reggie's party got broken up—everyone is coming here." Within minutes, the backyard was full of high-school students. I worked the keg and tried not to put too much foam in the glasses. The bouncers had already collected two hundred dollars and after the cost of the kegs we were at least a hundred dollars ahead. I took shots of tequila from a bottle someone passed around. Someone was blasting The Cure's album "Standing on a Beach" and a group of kids were singing along to "Boys Don't Cry."

By eleven, the backyard was overflowing. The bouncers were drunk and had stopped taking money. The party had moved inside. I felt as if I was walking through a kaleidoscope of people. I thought, *What are all these people doing in the house?* Tracy ran up to me and grabbed my arm. "Waa-Waa, it's the police," she slurred. "They want to talk to someone in charge."

I looked through the front window and saw four cop cars in the driveway. I shook myself to clear my head and walked outside with Tracy. An officer walked up to me and said, "Do you live here?" "Yes," I said in my oldest-child voice.

The officer shined a flashlight into my eyes. I felt myself wobble in my monkey boots. "Are you intoxicated, young lady?" he asked. Tracy whimpered beside me. "No, I'm fine." I said, and shrugged my shoulders. The officer lectured me. "We've had several complaints from your neighbors. Everyone needs to leave. We could arrest you for underage drinking."

I turned my head and watched as the police ushered a line of people out of the backyard into the street. "Get a move on," the police yelled through bullhorns. Someone screamed, "Go, Juanita! Tell those pigs off!"

"Why are you shutting down the party?" I asked. "This is fucking ridiculous, it's only eleven-thirty," I said as I got in the officer's face. "Fuck off!" I shouted, the tequila making me brave.

Tracy tried to calm me down, but I pushed her arm away. She turned and walked into the house. After the cops left, I found her hiding in the closet, black eyeliner smeared all over her tear-streaked face. The cops didn't arrest me. They should have.

When Mom and Dad came home a couple of days later, the neighbors had signed a petition to have us evicted.

Yes, throwing the party was stupid. Yes, it was wrong. Yes, my parents suffered for it. Yet, somehow, it all seems fitting.

Bad Things Happen

I don't like to talk about bad things. I would rather just drink and party. Or better yet, take me to a concert and I'll lose myself there. When I saw The Smiths live in concert, I thought I was going to pop like a balloon from the pure joy of it. It was one of the best days of my life. Morrissey was so beautiful up on stage, and his voice echoed and stirred something in me. He made me feel sad and happy at the same time.

It was my senior year of high school and we were living in Ontario. The rental house was right below Fourth Street by Yum Yum Donuts, the place where Dad got day-old donuts on Sundays. I remember that house because it's where I crashed my first car, and where Dad ran over our cat, and where we had our legendary kegger party. It was also where Dad almost killed himself.

I don't know when Dad got the call that evening. It was still light out when I came home from school and Dad was crying. His oldest daughter Barbara, our half-sister, had died in a horrific head-on collision. Barbara was Dad's daughter from his first marriage to a woman called Tiny. He had lost custody of Barbara and her younger sister Roberta when they were little. Barbara had been living in the trailer park my parents managed, but when Dad lost the bar, Barbara moved to Oregon with her girls Rosie, Desiree, and baby Sara in tow.

Mom always said Barbara was unlucky in love and that all of her kids had different fathers. Barbara's younger sister Roberta, who Mom called the responsible one, had been married for years, and lived in Kansas with her husband and two sons.

Dad loved Barbara more than anything in the world. Mom said it was because Barbara needed him the most. It made Mom angry that Dad would do anything for Barbara. He would drive for hours to help her if she was stuck somewhere.

Mom, who never called in sick to work, had decided not to go in that day. She was there when Dad locked himself in the bathroom. Dad sounded like a wounded animal, screaming "Barbara! My Barbara!" again and again.

We all huddled in the hallway by the bathroom listening as Dad howled out his sorrow. After a while, I couldn't take it anymore and I sat in my room covering my ears.

Mom was pounding on the door.

"John, open the door," she said over and over. "Please, John."

Mom wasn't mad for once, and she was calm and kind. That was what scared me. I ran over and started crying and begging him, "Please, Dad, open the door, please!"

"John, we love you," Mom said into the door over and

over, almost like a prayer.

Dad kept repeating Barbara's name, over and over. He wouldn't stop crying.

Mom whispered in my ear, "Dad has his gun in there with him."

"Barb, Barb!" Dad wailed.

"John, open the door, please," Mom cried.

Dad cried, "No." He was sobbing, "I don't want to be here anymore, not without Barb."

I don't remember how long he was in there exactly, but it felt like forever and a day. I don't remember what finally persuaded him to come out of the bathroom.

That night, I put on the Go-Go's *Vacation* and played the song "Worlds Away" on repeat over and over, until I fell asleep.

Later, Dad and Mom took one last drive for Barbara. Dad scraped together every cent he had to bury Barbara and buy her a headstone in Oregon. He had the headstone inscribed with the words "Loving mother and daughter." Something changed in Dad after Barbara died.

Under the Big Black Sun

It is graduation day, and instead of sitting on the graduation field with my twin sister Jackie and bestie Tracy, I am sitting in the bleachers with Mom, Dad, and my little sister Annie, who is now sixteen and a sophomore. I should be on the field graduating, too, but I threw it all away. I partied and dozed away my senior year. I went from goody-two-shoes, straight-A student to punk-rock high-school dropout. It only took me months to ruin my life.

Years later, I will think that maybe it was predestined to end up that way.

My favorite uncle, Tio Roland (who's a dead ringer for Wolfman Jack) is also here, down from Orange County, to watch Jackie walk. His van has a scene from Hawaii painted on the side. Tio Roland refuses to look at me. When Jackie walks up in her graduation cap and gown, he says, "Congratulations, mija" in his gravelly voice and hands her fifty dollars. She beams at him.

I look up into the sky and blink into the sun.

Tio Roland is my godfather and our favorite uncle. Jackie had only inherited Roland after her godfather, my dad's obese Montana cousin Mickey, died on an operating table. We are made to share Roland as a godfather, like we share everything else in our life as twins.

Mom says I broke her heart by dropping out. Dad says she was crying all week. But today she is angry. She had begged me to stay in school, but I wouldn't listen.

I look into Mom's red-rimmed eyes and remember when I was little, sitting at the dining-room table, her teaching me to read. "C'mon, Jenny, sound it out."

I remember how kind and sweet Mom was to me, so patient, reading me the words, giving me the gift of the one thing that would sustain me, the ability to read. Mom always said that she didn't want me to end up as a waitress like her. I was going to college. That's why she taught me to read when I was three.

I picture Mom taking me to the library every weekend when I was a kid. She would always say, "Get as many books as you can, Jenny." I remember Mom arguing to have Jackie and me skip third grade after pestering our elementary-school administration to test and enroll us in GATE, the program for gifted and talented exceptional students. I remember when I was in junior high, eating at Mom's work and listening to her bragging to a fellow waitress, "Jenny loves to read. She'll read a cereal box if that's all she has."

I remember my parents waving my straight-A report card around to all their friends and Mom's relatives. I picture Mom and Dad in the stands at my swim meets, they came whenever they could get a Saturday off, cheering me on.

"Mom," I say. I swallow the lump in my throat. She turns her head.

I look at Roland with shiny eyes and think, *Say something*.

Roland just shakes his head.

Dad grunts and mutters, "Judy, go easy on her" and puts his hand on my shoulder. I jerk away. Dad looks at me with a hurt look in his blue eyes. He is wearing his usual jean shirt with a bolo tie and his Wranglers with his Big John belt buckle. Mom's hair curls around her face and she is wearing a lace dress. She still refuses to look at me.

I messed everything up.

Did Mom think I wanted this to happen? I was the one that was supposed to go to Claremont McKenna. She always said I was the smartest. But I stopped going to school senior year. I slept all day and drank all night.

I think it was the culmination of everything. All of the childhood chaos, and Dad losing his bar, and then Mom and Dad losing the house. My job at Round Table did not help. I stayed after work to drink every night. Of course, there were bright points: music, parties, ditching in Hollywood, and concert after concert. Those things were more of an escape really.

The worst day was the day our half-sister Barb died in a car accident. That weekend, I got shit-faced with all my friends, numbing myself as usual.

The worst part is that it was never a conscious decision to drop out. Instead, it was just one small decision after another that added up to me becoming a dropout.

I remember Mom saying there was no money for college. I had no idea about student loans. I just gave up.

It was easier to sleep all day than trying to make my way through the darkness. I felt as if I was in a dark cave with no exit. The truth was, I had been fighting depression for years. All of my chickens were finally coming home to roost.

Senior year, I would pretend to go to school by getting dressed and walking out the door. I would sneak back once Mom left for her job on the breakfast shift and crawl into bed.

Soon, I stopped caring if Mom knew.

"Jenny, get up!" she would yell, throwing water on me.

I would scream back, "Just leave me alone."

Even Jackie, who was struggling with her own issues, told me to get it together. "What are you doing? You just need to finish. It's one class, Jenny," Jackie said with an exasperated look in her eyes.

Today, I know I have disappointed everyone.

Back in the bleachers, I look at my dad. He shakes his head. "It's OK, Jenny, you'll finish, you're a smart girl," he says. "Thanks, Dad," I say, patting his hand.

Refusing to look at my mom, I turn and walk away from everyone. I go hide underneath the bleachers, where it is dark and smells like piss.

The environment matches my mood, and tears drip on my cigarette. I take drag after drag until my cigarette is a tiny nub that burns my fingers. At least I am feeling something. I feel as if I haven't felt anything in years.

Tears are running from my eyes. My thick black eyeliner is smearing all over my face, and I wipe at my kohl-lined eyes with the edge of my Sex Pistols tee.

My head pounds and I rub my temples, and try to hiccup my tears away. I wipe at my eyes again and think, what a screw-up I am.

I can't stop weeping.

I think of being at the Hollywood Palladium seeing The Smiths and how I screamed with joy.

When Jackie's name is called, I flinch and I know that I can't watch. Look, I know that I should go out into the sun and watch her walk.

Mom says we had our own language as kids. I picture me and Jackie as kids on the playground. I remember her sticking up for me and me for her. Putting out fires together, navigating our crazy childhood. Jackie and I are supposed to be walking that field together.

Back under the bleachers, I know I should be happy for Jackie—she's my Wonder Twin and all. But I can't be happy, and I bury my head in my arms. I can't stop crying. I am not a cool punk-rock girl anymore; it was all just an act.

I am a fucking loser.

It's all coming out of me, like water from a broken tap.

I hear the school band start playing, and the music echoes in my ears as I stare down at the concrete beneath my feet. I think, *My life is over*.

Suddenly, I remember sitting at the park when I was little and how I would always wonder, *Is everyone's life like this?* I always took a book to the park when Mom kicked us out of the house when she couldn't find Dad, which was often.

I remember all of the books I read, some of them by flashlight, and how I would squint into them and lose myself. I read *Gone with the Wind* over and over, along with F. Scott Fitzgerald, Judy Blume, S.E. Hinton and, of course, Mom's Harlequin romance novels.

Those books meant everything to me. They saved me and showed me the possibilities of life.

Then punk and post-punk music came into my life and changed everything again. I found a place I could go to with all of my sadness. That music showed me that there was life after darkness.

My favorite Smiths song "There is a Light That Never Goes Out" whispers in my head. Lighting another cigarette, I take drag after drag.

Did I want to die?

I wipe at my face and shake my head.

I decide at that moment that I want to live. I want out of this piss-ant town. I want to prove myself to everyone who has given me up for dead.

All is not lost, I just need a plan. How can I get out of here? There has to be a way. I tell myself, *You will be OK. Tomorrow is another day.*

Epilogue Part One

Trailer Park Daze

Waking up, I stretch and cover my ears. Mom and Dad are up and already arguing. I moved back home with them into their trailer last week.

First, my car blew up. Then, Adrian and I broke up. Next, I lost my waitressing job after I called in sick. My boss's big blonde-haired head had always hated me. She just needed an excuse to fire me. Now all I had left was my bagel job three days a week, where I had to wake up at five a.m. to make six bucks an hour.

There's also my illustrious junior college career. I was just appointed editor-in-chief of *The Mountaineer*, Mount SAC's newspaper. It's one of the few good things right now. Most days, I feel like I will never get out of junior college hell. In twenty years, I'll probably be forty still living in my parents' trailer trying to pass my math class. (I dropped Algebra 2 again. I fucking hate math. There is something about numbers that give me a headache. I transpose them. I like words. Paragraphs. Layout. Stories.)

Dad yells from the kitchen. "Jenny, I made you some fried bologna and eggs."

The trailer park my parents live in is in Pomona, on Mission Boulevard, in the worst part of town. I never thought I would live in a trailer, much less back with my mom and dad, but I didn't have any other options after I lost my apartment. After not being able to make my rent, I came home, tail between my legs, back to broke-down crazy town. When I moved out of my parent's house, I said I would never go back.

Yet, here I lay. On a twin bed, in a trailer, with a tapestry of dogs playing poker staring at me.

"Jenny, your eggs are getting cold," Dad says, his head peeking through the door. He's already dressed, wearing his usual blue Wrangler jeans with his Big John belt buckle and his cowboy shirt. At least he left off the bolo tie.

I get up reluctantly. I could sleep all day; it is only seven in the morning.

"Finally up?" Mom says as I walk into the kitchen to wolf down my breakfast. She has her usual cup of coffee in her hand. She is probably on her fifth cup.

"Yes, Mom. I have class at ten."

I look at her with my leave-me-alone face.

Mom mutters to herself as she walks out of the room. Soon, I hear the front door slam.

Thank God she is gone. I don't know which one is worse. Dad with all his pandering and hugs or Mom with her screaming and yelling. She is always angry. Mad at me. Mad at Dad that she has to go to work at the restaurant while he lays around the house on disability. Dad would rather be working than be here at home, but he can't. All those years of moving furniture broke him physically.

Shit, I have a newspaper story to get out today. My favorite part about being a journalist is bringing the tape recorder and interviewing someone, and listening and taking notes. I can't help but take notes; it helps me listen. I have my mom's short attention span, and my focus only kicks in when my hands are moving.

I rush into the shower. The bathroom is filthy. Actually, the entire trailer is dirty, with shit everywhere, and the whole place reeks of cigarette smoke. Even my books smell like smoke. I am taking a Shakespeare class, and the moment I walk into the classroom, people wrinkle their noses from the overwhelming stench of Dad's Kent cigarettes on my clothes.

I get dressed. T-shirt, jeans. No makeup. I put a beanie on so I don't have to wash my hair. It smells like smoke, too.

"Dad, you ready?" I yell out the bathroom door.

"Let me finish this game," Dad yells back.

He is playing his Yahtzee computer handheld. He plays the game all day. Mom got it for him to keep him from going to the casino and losing all their rent money. I guess the game is better than nothing.

The Talking Heads' song "Once in a Lifetime" floats into my mind. I take a deep breath, in and out. I walk outside and look at the row of trailers, lined up like rectangular boxes. This trailer park is so depressing, nothing like the house we had when I was little.

Back then, we each had our own room and a swimming pool. My parents lost the nice house along with my dad's bar when I was in high school. I wanted to attend Claremont McKenna, but I made my proverbial bed when I dropped out of high school senior year, five units short of a diploma.

So yes, just call me class of nineteen-eighty-nine high-school dropout loser.

I open the door to Dad's maroon Baretta and place my backpack in the back seat on top of a pile of *Reader's Digest* magazines. Dad loves his *Reader's Digest* and *TV Guides*. They are everywhere. The car's ashtray is overflowing so I dump it in the trash outside. Dad walks outside and lights up a cigarette as he gets in the car. There is no use complaining about him smoking; I'm just lucky I don't have to take the bus. Dad turns on the country station. Johnny Cash's "I Walk the Line" wafts in the air.

As he pulls away from the trailer, I open up my Shakespeare book and start reading. I am transported into *As You Like It*. Some days I feel like Rosalind, always pretending to be someone else.

After my head spins, I stop reading. Carsick.

"Proud of you, Jenny. For going to school and all that work on the paper," Dad says with a smile and his signature wink. "I know it's not easy."

I smile back at him. I wipe tears from my eyes, and roll down my window to breathe in the wind.

Years later, while on hospice care and as he lay dying from pancreatic cancer, Dad would say once again, "Jenny, I am so proud of you." He would add, "Take care of your mom for me, Jenny. She loves you girls so very much."

So I do.

The Mantz family: John, Jackie, Annie, Juanita and Judy

Poems

David

Your name was David.

Mom says I look just like you.

So true.

You were born at five a.m. in the hospital

by Knott's Berry Farm when it was still a farm.

She held you in her arms, amazed

at how peacefully you slept,

and how you never cried that day.

Later, they would tell her that you were born deaf.

No one knew how or why it happened.

You slowly grew up in your silent world.

When you walked you never

heard your own steps.

When you turned five,

Mom moved you to Oregon for deaf school.

On a rainy winter night,

she left you with friends and

sat alone at a bar in Portland.

She met a man—and after two weeks,

moved in with him.

One night when he didn't come home
she decided to find him.
Walking from bar to bar,
she held your yellow-mitten-covered hand.
In the dusk, at the corner,
you broke away as kids will do.
You could not hear her screams.
A car skidded on the wet road.
It took your life.
She will blame the man she was searching for.
My father.

The Plastic Cheese and Me: Part I

It sat in the park,
a vision of orangeness and scratched-up youth.
The maze looked hard and inviting
like a large candied fruit.
I would often hide inside its twisting, holed walls.
Its smell was unpleasant,
whiffs of urine dried by sun.
Its broad cover afforded sanctuary for one.
Oh, the Plastic Cheese. I remember it well.
A snug place to hide from all the screams
and the shouts.

The Plastic Cheese and Me: Part II

The Plastic Cheese now sits forlorn
on dried, lonely grass,
a rusty swing set its only companion.
Do you remember?
We used to go there.
Mom would have one of her fits
and scream "Get the fuck out!"
as Dad perched on a barstool miles away
waving his glass,
while us three walked the block to the park
in the dark.
I would huddle inside the Plastic Cheese
watching you swing, until we heard Mom's
pleading shouts echo over the rooftops
and around the corner.
The wind lifting her voice in the air for us.
"Girls..., come back."

Shit on a Shingle (A Waitressing Moniker)

You tell the waitress, "Over easy, please."
You ask her for coffee: "No cream. No sugar."
You watch her stoop and bend to clean the booth.
Her hands shake pouring the coffee,
liver spots line her arms,
hair pulled back in a fitting bun,
red shirt stained with butter and crumbs.
The waitress smiles as she walks past.
You remind her of her daughter,
the one in law school,
the one her regulars all know.
You're in a hurry, on the run.
You snap your fingers, wave your hands.
Treat her as if she does not exist,
except to serve you.
Your shitty breakfast.

Juanita Mantz

Father O' Mine: Part I

I stopped by your apartment today.
You sat listless on your cigarette-holed sofa.
Mom yelled at you to put some clothes on.
"Dammit, John, don't sit in your underwear all day!"
Still, every morning you prick your finger.
Checking your sugar level,
trying in your own way to survive.
You say I don't understand what it's like.
To sit alone all day with nothing to do.
You applied at the local Walmart store.
They didn't want you, not even for a greeter.
You spend your monthly Social Security check
at the local casinos:
Agua Caliente, San Manuel, and Morongo.
You drop your first quarter in the slot,
pulling the long silver handle,
waiting for the three sevens: all in a row.

Red, white, and blue.

Steel Frame

The hospital bed came today.
A fat man named Lenny brought it in,
all shiny steel and brand-new.
Trapeze bar hanging from its right side
looked out of place.
Just weeks ago you were walking,
driving yourself to the casinos.
Now you just lay there,
small, shrunken version of your former self,
yellowed by liver tumors.
I sit up with you all night
propping my pillow next to your bed,
studying the fine lines and wrinkles.
You moan in your sleep.
I commit it all to memory.
You wake me up at three a.m. screaming.
A man—"a passerby"—is standing at your bed.
I tell you that no one is there.
That everything is OK.
I am not so sure.

The River Card

I used to always complain
you only wanted to go the casinos
or to the race track.
Never for Thai food. No sushi.
"Take me to the Bicycle Club,
watch me play Texas Hold 'Em.
The buy-in is only forty."

But I would never take you.
Instead, we would meet for breakfast.
It was always short, only an hour.
Not much of a conversation starter,
you would sit and eat your hash and eggs.
Sometimes I would scowl at you
if you breathed heavily at the table.

Now everything has changed.
I wonder if I close my eyes,
if I wish hard enough,
can I sit with you at that poker table,
drinking, waiting for the river card?
Instead of sitting with you
by your hospital bed?

Oxygen

I turned on my video camera late last night.
Looked at your swollen legs,
watched your drawn face saying "I love you."
Pressing rewind again and again
until my finger was bruised.

I want to erase the last two months.
To have you with me once again.
I would just sit quietly beside you.
It seems impossible that I can see you.
Looking at your face—that face—

my heart feels swollen, covered in moss,
suffocated by sorrow. Like a bird
whose tiny heart has stopped beating.
I can't breathe
because breathing means living.

And you're dead.

Father O' Mine: Part II

Now that you're gone
Some days your image comes
Upon me like lightning.
On the subway
Balancing in three-inch heels
Walking down the hill
For a cup of coffee
I am back in your arms
Sitting next to you lounging
In your blue La-Z-Boy recliner.
In Yosemite, all of us camping out
You clean the fish
Frying it over the campfire.
That Vegas trip when I was twenty-two
In that horrible Winnebago
The one that broke down by the state line.
I want to save that image of you
As a confident cowboy
Who would let me help shift the gears
On your eighteen-wheeler while you drove
Smoking your Kent cigarette
One hand on the wheel

Johnny Cash on the stereo
Picture of your family in your pocket.
That's who you were
That's who you are
Father of mine

IPod

(San Francisco)

Walking through the subway
I feel invincible,
Not at all like my normal self.
The white headphones signify my ascent
into a club of sorts. The epitome of coolness
I tap my feet on the escalator

Humming.

It feels good to be distant
Lost in the sound of bass and drum
I smile—no longer anxious
No need to meet other eyes
My audio sunglasses
Bathe me in blissful

Anonymity.

Do others feel this peaceful?
I know the immersion is an illusion
I am drowning
Feeling nothing
Except the rhythms
Running in my head, fast

Slow.

I am addicted. I switch from
White Stripes to Miss Dynamite
To Aimee Mann
To my high-school days
With a little of the Pixies,
Erasure, then some Cure,

Joy Division.

I feel like a teenager again.
Hanging out in the quad
Smoking stale cigarettes
Stolen from my dad
Wanting to be someone
Anyone, but me.

Blue.

Black hair, stud earring in one nostril
Before that was overdone
Bright red thermals cover legs
I will always be ashamed of
Only later will I see this
As a costume

Masquerade.

Designed to hide
The pure sadness of that time
To obscure the goals I had abandoned
In hopelessness by age sixteen.
I want to yell
"Girl, all is not lost"

No.

Years will be lost
Drinking, trying to dull
The sharpness of it all
Somehow, some way
I will emerge
Defiant and proving wrong

All.

Who had given me up
For dead. A high-school
Dropout, a statistic
But never humble, I knew
I was powerful and equal
To all of them.

Regardless.

Here I am walking
To the beats in my head
My feet pounding
The moving sidewalk
Suddenly I can't suppress
The urge to run.

Bathroom Tile

I wish I could send an airplane
to write overhead, *He is dead*.
The funeral was not enough,
not nearly enough.
I wanted to say goodbye in a grand way, with fanfare.
I have watched too many movies
and maybe expect too much. I thought death
would be peaceful, his eyes would close slowly, and
I would watch as his soul left his body.

It was not like that at all.
It happened in an instant, the minute I turned.
They tried to resuscitate.
Their futile efforts seemed so profane.
All alone, his swollen naked body beseeched me:
Make the right decision.
"No more. He's gone."
The chaos of that day haunts me and his blood remains
on the tile of the bathroom floor.

I don't have the strength to clean it up.

Epilogue Part Two

Home

My sisters and I planned my dad's funeral. My mom was in shock. She didn't talk much, but she started hugging me and telling me she loved me. She never ever did that before. My dad's death had changed her. It had changed all of us. It had changed me most of all. I was transformed, transported and mutated into a different me.

Looking through his closet, I picked out my dad's favorite blue cowboy shirt and bolo tie for him to wear in the casket. I went through all of his man jewelry. Mom let me have a turquoise eagle bolo tie of his and the hat I had bought for him in Ireland, the one he wore religiously, that had an Irish prayer in the lining. We used the Irish prayer on his funeral pamphlet.

The day of the funeral was overcast. The X song "Please Come Back to Me" swam in my head over and over, as if on repeat on the radio.

The services were in Colton. Annie's godfather Manuel, a deacon, presided over it. We had pictures of my dad from when he was a young man in Montana with Roberta and Barbara and then later, pictures with Mom and us girls. Jackie made a collage. Deacon Manuel talked about how he and my dad would drink beers together.

As I sat through the services, I couldn't help remembering how bad that last day with him was. I didn't want to remember that day or him on the floor, or the paramedics working on him.

I wanted to remember my dad as he was, driving his truck with one hand on the wheel, country music blasting on the stereo. How he loved making us girls giggle when he let us use his CB radio.

Johnny Cash's "Daddy Sang Bass" filled the funeral home right before I gave the eulogy.

I read his eulogy, a story I wrote about my dad taking us to the drive-in movie theater when we were little kids.

My voice broke at the end. Jackie spoke next. We played some more country songs, including "The Gambler" by Kenny Rogers.

It didn't look like him in the casket. People always say that about their loved ones but, I mean, it didn't look like him at all. He was motionless and gray. My dad was always smiling and laughing even when he was limping around in pain during his last days. He had a kindness to him that radiated. He was everything. He made me the people person I am. He was all heart. He was the sun.

Dad would sometimes tell me, "One day I'll be gone and you'll miss me more than you can imagine, Jenny." He was right, I did. I thought about how much time I had missed with my dad by being gone for so long. I thought about when he and my mom came out to Texas. We drove out to Louisiana and spent the night on a riverboat casino. My dad stayed up all night gambling in the poker room, and I wish I would've sat with him playing Texas Hold 'Em.

At the end of my dad's funeral, we played the Beatles "Here Comes the Sun." My eyes burned with unshed tears, and suddenly I started weeping, until I couldn't weep anymore.

The days after the funeral were surreal. My body felt numb most days, and for weeks I walked around in a daze. Beer helped until it didn't.

Everything had changed.

For some reason, I knew couldn't go back to my life to San Francisco. I needed to be home, back in the Inland Empire. I quit the San Francisco law firm right after the funeral, wishing I had quit and moved back home years before. Before it was too late. Before my dad was gone.

We moved out of our San Francisco apartment and Adrian found a single room to rent to finish up his last year in dental school in San Francisco. I don't remember much from that time. I can't remember how I made the decision to move. Or how I packed everything up. Most days, I was just so damn sad. My heart felt like it was a piece of concrete that would burst out of my chest. The days went by. Life happened. My legs felt like lead, weighed down with grief.

A recruiter found me yet another law firm job, this one in Riverside, and I moved in with Jackie in Colton. Jackie was teaching high school in San Bernardino. We still fought like cats and dogs, but even the arguments were somewhat comforting. It felt like home. Most nights, I couldn't sleep and would sit in bed and stare at the ceiling. On the weekends, I spent time with my mom and sisters and reconnected with my best friends Tracy and Melinda.

After working for the law firm for a little more than a year and a half, I realized I was done with corporate litigation and big firm life. I interviewed at the public defender's office in Riverside and was offered a job. My first day at work, I knew I had made the right decision. The day I started as a deputy public defender was like the day I wrote my first story; I knew it was meant to be.

In my new job, I would find myself representing the most mentally ill clientele, and I realized that I was good at it. I always say, I can do crazy, I just can't do sane. I found a way to connect with the law again by fighting for the least fortunate, and I always understood what my clients meant when they said they didn't have a ride or money for lunch. As a deputy public defender, I tried to help them and give them some hope. My job was to help them navigate a broken system with some grace. Fighting for them gave me a purpose that had been lacking in my civil litigation career.

On the weekends, I started writing stories about my childhood, and the stories gushed out. Story after story came to me. I did summer writing workshops at VONA and Macondo and they loved my memoir pieces, especially the ones in child voice.

Whenever I wrote, I could hear my dad's voice echoing in my mind as I put pen to page.

Soon, I started listening to all of my favorite music from when I was a teenager. I brought out my combat boots and did my eyes like Siouxsie again. I went to concerts again. We saw The Cure, The Pixies, X, Morrissey, Buzzcocks, and more. At the concerts, I sang myself hoarse, jumping up and down to my favorite music. I was finding joy again and myself in the process.

Adrian finished dental school and moved back to Southern California, and we got married at the courthouse in a civil ceremony with his parents and my mom. I thought of my dad the entire day. Every time he entered my head, I teared up. Then, finally, I just smiled and looked up at the big bar in the sky, hoping silently that my dad was sitting on a barstool, waving his glass in the air, toasting us.

My mom and I became good friends. She moved in with me for a time. I made her retire from waitressing and eventually she moved to a senior community mere miles away. My sisters and I bonded and became even closer. Dad would have been so proud to see that I was me again. Jenny was back.

Adrian and I bought a house in San Bernardino, less than twenty miles from where I grew up. I was no longer running. I was finally home. Home is where I would stay (to this very day).

The End

Dad's Eulogy

My father loved movies.
I mean he really loved movies.
He took me to see all of my favorites:
Jaws, ET, Star Wars, Superman, Rocky,
The Bad News Bears,
Escape from Witch Mountain, and *Little Darlings.*
My mother worked weekend nights waiting tables.
Dad would take me and my sisters to the drive-in.
Before we left, he would pop up a big bag of popcorn,
and I mean a big bag, those brown, hard paper bags
they used to give you at the supermarket.
Dad would double-bag the popcorn
and then melt down a stick of margarine,
pouring it in straight from the pan, adding lots of salt.
At the drive-in, we would sit on lawn chairs brought from
home
and listen to the static-filled speakers, not saying a word,
occasionally sticking our hands into the brown bag,
wiping our oil-stained fingers on our bare legs.
My father would never make us leave early.
We would sit and watch the credits of the last movie roll
before he started up his old ratty pickup truck to take us
home.
We all had a stomachache from the popcorn.
It was worth it.

Afterword

It is very hard to write scene-by-scene memoir. It is why many fictionalize their lives, as James Joyce did in *A Portrait of the Artist as a Young Man*.

This book is my attempt to capture that which cannot be captured or re-created and to take it to a higher place. I have to say, I have done my best to capture my truth and to depict what happened in my childhood scene by scene.

I must acknowledge, however, that memory is fallible. My process for writing is to get into a writing space in my head, almost a trance, and then I write trying to remember those times vividly. Is the dialogue an exact re-creation of what was said? Perhaps not always—and some details and events have been compressed and, at times, altered and reordered—but all I can say is that it is what I remember it as. In some ways, I don't know what to call this.

All I can say is that I have done my best to capture the truth—again, my truth and only mine—of my childhood and to confirm details when I could. I do not write in figurative language. I don't have the skill to make everything poetic. I leave that to my twin sister Jackie, who is also a writer and who has written about our family from her perspective in a much different, very lovely and lyrical style. There will also be some disagreement about some of these stories. My sister Annie asserts to this day that she was not favored. But these are my stories to tell here and I am sticking with my version of the stories. Memories and perspectives differ. Still, these are my memories and my story, told in my way.

After my dad died, I finally began to get to know and understand my mom. We've become very close friends and I so admire her. She's a fighter and an independent person. She would do anything for me and I would do anything for her.

Looking back, I feel sorry for what my mom went through back when I was a kid. She was always exhausted. Her anger came from dealing with financial stress and a husband that loved to drink, all while trying to care for three kids born within 16 months of each other. When I first started writing, my dad was the hero, but after years of working on this book, I have finally realized—and perhaps that's why this book took over fifteen years to finish—that my mom was the one who kept it all together.

My mom was the one who taught me to read when I was three, sounding out words at a small kitchen table, and the one who took me to the library and stressed the value of an education. My mom was the one who always bought us nice clothes. Ultimately, my mom was, and is, a heroine of sorts and the one who corralled my dreamer, Don Quixote–type father, who was always chasing windmills. Eventually, I realized that it was my mom that was the thread holding the torn blanket of our family together and that my dad was no prince, but more of a hard-drinking and lovable rascal frog.

My mom loved my dad to distraction and, although many years have passed since he died, she rarely lets a day go by without mentioning him. She will say fondly, "I miss your dad. He drove me crazy, but I loved him so much.... Still do."

Reading first saved me as a child and then as a young adult. As a child, I was a very eclectic reader, having read my mom's library of Harlequin romance novels, the *Little House on the Prairie* books, and *Gone with the Wind* multiple times. I remember my elementary-school teacher being shocked that my vocabulary included the word *ravished*. Judy Blume's books were also an integral part of my childhood. I devoured her books. I would read them over and over, imagining myself into her stories. It could be why I always envisioned this memoir as dialogue and character driven. Jenny as a character is very much a Sally J. Freedman type of character. As a kid, I was always daydreaming and making up stories, stories starring myself, in my head. Later, I would read Sandra Cisneros' *House on Mango Street* and James Joyce's *Dubliners*.

My love of the written word will, once again, save my life when I am a depressed and stressed-out lawyer working long hours at a large law firm in Texas. Looking out of my high-rise Houston office at night, poems will start pouring out of me. Then, when my dad dies, writing will come along to save me once again. This book is the result.

Juanita Mantz: USC Law School Commencement
Ceremony, May 20, 2002

Acknowledgements

There are so many people and organizations to thank so please forgive me if I miss anyone.

First, to Frank Kearns at Los Nietos Press. Thank you for believing in me, and for giving me the time and space I needed to finish this manuscript the way it deserved. Thank you for the hard work on editing and production to make this book beautiful. You are all heart and soul and you made this book, and my dream, come true.

Thank you to Mark Givens and Dennis Callaci for publishing my first chapbook about public defense and punk rock. I'm eternally grateful for your friendship. You helped start the magical journey I'm on.

Thanks to VONA and all its members and teachers, especially, Elmaz Abinader, Faith Adiele, Andrew Pham, Minal Hajratwala and David Mura, all who kept me believing. And to my special VONA peeps Samuel Autman, Rowena Cruz, and Lucy Rodriguez-Hanley.

Gratitude to the Macondo Writers Workshop, an organization I found through my IE girl and fellow writer, manuscript reader and dear friend, Macondista liz gonzález. I am eternally grateful to liz, who has been with me on this journey and always supported my work, and to Macondistas Joy Castro, Stephanie Elizondo Griest, Pat Alderete, Cecilia Balli, Allison Hedge Coke and Leticia Del Toro for all their support and kindness. And especially for Sandra Cisneros who started it all.

Much thanks to the University of New Orleans and the students and faculty in my MFA program who gave me valuable feedback, especially my professors, Richard Goodman and Juyanne James.

Thank you to Brett Paesel for her teaching and friendship. Thank you to Marilyn Friedman at Writing Pad.

To my Tres Libras writing group, Lynda Hoggan and Frances Borella who spent years reading my stories. Our monthly meetings were my lifeline.

Thank you to the Inlandia Institute, and to all of the board and its members, but especially to Executive Director Cati Porter for all her support. Thank you also to Shawna-Lee I. Perrin and Hồng-Mỹ Basrai.

For Jo Scott Coe and Stephanie Barbé Hammer, two of the best teachers and mentors a girl could ever ask for.

Thank you to Macondista/VONA alum and IE girl, Cassandra Lopez for publishing my first story. Thank you to Ruth Nolan for her support, encouragement and for facilitating one of the first workshops I attended at Inlandia.

Special thanks to my UCR besties and fellow writers Gina Devore and Emily Fernandez.

Thank you to Elsa Valmidiano for her support and friendship.

Thank you to Michelle Cruz Gonzales, the ultimate punkera, for all her reading and encouragement and to Michelle Villegas Threadgold for her belief in me.

For all the deputy public defenders, and those in our writing group years ago, Jennifer Bender, Sandra Bisignani, Maggie Cohen and Brianne King. And to Barbara Plate, Monica Ngyuen, Judith Gweon and Jen Small for their support.

For my rockstar podcast producer April Duran.

For all the librarians. And for my professors who pushed me to write, especially, Holly Cannon and Tiffany Lopez.

To my best friend Tracy Sauls aka Tra Tra. Thank you for always being my biggest cheerleader. I'm so grateful I met you all those decades ago at Chaffey, my story would not be the same without you. Besties forever! We will be blue haired old ladies, still dancing.

To my best friend Melinda Terrazas. Thank you for being my best friend. All our great times made my life an adventure. Hanging out with you feels like home. I love you Mel!

To my big sister Roberta. You are such a part of this story. Daddy would be so proud of how close we are. Thanks to Cousin Pascale too.

Thank you especially to my twin sister Jackie Mantz, who's also my wonder twin and a wonderful writer who has a doctorate in education. We are always linked. I so admire you and love you. Always. Thanks to my little sis Annie who still takes care of everyone. I love you both and am so grateful for your support. This book was not easy and went through many versions, some of which were difficult to read or hear. I hope, finally, after years of writing this, that I got it right.

To my niece Selena, thank you for being you. To my niece and goddaughter Sophie, I love you. Be good, but have adventures too. Much love to my nephew Nicolas.

Thank you to my husband and my soul mate, Dr. Adrian Pelaez, who had to put up with my early AM writing practice for so many years. Thank you for always knowing that I could finish this book and for allowing me the time and space to write. You gave me "a room of my own".

For my mother-in-law Orieta and for the dearly departed, my

father-in-law Alberto and brother-in-law Gabe.

For Frodo and Chewbacca, my fur kids. You know.

To my mom Juliana ("Judy") Mantz, you're one of my best friends. Thank you for loving me. For doing everything for me. Always. You inspire me. You're my shero.

To my dear dad John W. Mantz, Jr., I hope you know, I did it all for you. I miss you every day, more than words can ever say. You were right, I sure do miss you now that you're gone...

About the Author

Juanita E. Mantz ("JEM") is a deputy public defender, writer, performer and podcaster, one who believes that stories have the power to change the world. She graduated from UCR in 1999 with a Bachelor's in English Literature and received her J.D. from USC Law in 2002. She is in the low residency MFA creative writing program at The University of New Orleans.

Juanita has been with the Law Offices of the Public Defender in Riverside County for over 13 years.

She is an alumna of VONA and The Macondo Writers Workshop and serves as Vice President on the Board of Directors of the Inlandia Institute. She has been published widely, including in *The Acentos Review, Aljazerra, As/Us, The Dirty Spoon, Entropy, Inlandia, MUSE, Riverside Press*

Enterprise, and *"San Bernardino, Singing,"* among others.

Juanita performed in the 2016 cast of Listen to Your Mother, Burbank. She has presented at the UCR Punk Conference, AWP, and Beyond Baroque. She also produced and taught the ASA 2020 Freedom Course on Combatting Mass Incarceration. On her video "Life of JEM" podcast, she does live interviews with artists, wellness practitioners and writers.

Her first book, titled *Portrait of a Deputy Public Defender, or how I became a punk rock lawyer,* a hybrid chapbook in essays, memoir & poetry challenging mass incarceration polices, was released by Bamboo Dart Press in August 2021. Her Life of JEM podcast and blog is available on Facebook and on her author website at:

https://juanitaemantz.com/.

Find her on Twitter @lifeofjem and on Insta @lifeofjem1.

Also By Los Nietos Press

Acts of Contrition: Short Stories, Victoria Waddle (2021)

Behind the Red Curtain: a Memoir, Hồng-Mỹ Basrai (2020)

Dutch Girl from Jakarta: From Indonesian Concentration Camp to Freedom, Maria Zeeman (2019)

Star Chasing, Thomas R. Thomas *(2019)*

Dancing in the Santa Ana Winds: Poems y Cuentos New and Selected, liz gonzález (2018)

California Trees, Kit Courter (2018)

Wingless, Linda Singer (2017)

Sharing Stories: Global Voices Coming Together, Various Authors (2016)

The Beatle Bump, Clifton Snider (2016)

Yearlings, Frank Kearns (2015)

So Cali, Trista Dominqu (2015)

Persons of Interest, Lorine Parks (2015)

ABOUT
LOS NIETOS PRESS

Los Nietos Press is dedicated to the countless generations of people whose lives and labor created the world community that today spreads over the coastal floodplain known simply as Los Angeles.

We take our name from the Los Nietos Spanish land grant that was south and east of the downtown area. Our purpose is to serve local writers so they may share their words with many, in the form of tangible books that can be held and read and passed on. This written art form is one way we realize our common bonds and help each other discover what is meaningful in life.

LOS NIETOS PRESS
www.LosNietosPress.com
LosNietosPress@Gmail.com

CPSIA information can be obtained
at www.ICGtesting.com
Printed in the USA
LVHW090133181221
706498LV00004B/112